The Complete
Book of
Saltwater
Aquariums

The Complete
Book of
Saltwater
Aquariums

HOW TO EQUIP
AND MAINTAIN YOUR MARINE
AQUARIUM AND UNDERSTAND
ITS ECOLOGY

Robert A. Stevenson, Jr.

FUNK & WAGNALLS
New York

Library of Congress Cataloging in Publication Data
Stevenson, Robert A.
    The complete book of saltwater aquariums.
    Bibliography: p.
    1. Marine aquariums. I. Title.
SF457.1.S72   639'.34   73-21520
ISBN 0-308-10090-5

1 2 3 4 5 6 7 8 9 10

Contents

SECTION II

ECOLOGY OF MARINE FISHES IN THEIR
NATURAL ENVIRONMENTS

General
Introduction

Many people desire to keep marine fishes in aquariums. This desire runs from those who merely wish to enjoy the beauties and fascination on a personal basis to those who wish to do scientific research. The former type of person is usually happy if his marine aquarium is clean and pretty and the fish are reasonably colorful and at least are not sulking in a corner, ragged in appearance or dying. The latter wishes to have fish that look good because they are healthy and, therefore, must be performing both physiologically and behaviorally in a more or less normal fashion—a normal fashion for being in an aquarium, at least.

Only a few people achieve this goal. It is routine to buy or catch marine fishes, to put a great deal of time and money into setting up an aquarium, and then to stock it with fish that look fine for a while, but then sicken and die. The routine, when it is obvious that fish look or act sick, is to consult a book or the attendant in an aquarium shop and to start dumping chemicals into the water to make them well again. Most likely, the trouble becomes worse, or some new problem with the health of the fish arises which initiates another search for new chemicals, after excessive doses of the first ones have failed. And if the chemicals fail, then maybe the diet is to blame because after all, the fish are not eating. So, the diet is changed and the failure of this course is marked by the deadly accumulation of uneaten food, which lies unnoticed within shells or around the bases of the sunken ships and colored stones that help to make the aquarium a place of beauty. Or if this doesn't work, then maybe the water is bad and a transfusion is in order. So the aquarium is drained and the aquarist wades through the slop of salt water and shuffles the lights, pumps and extension cords that are waiting patiently to sink their electrical fangs into his arm when his wet and salty fingers bridge the necessary gaps. All his efforts may not be in vain, and for a while the creaks in his back from lugging the heavy buckets of water and sand and manhandling the dead weight of glass are forgotten. He has the momentary joy of achieving his goal. But, slowly, surely, the old ailments creep back defying all the efforts, the changes and the hopes, and the bitter realization comes that the fight must go on, and on, and on.

The reasons why vast amounts of time and effort put into attempting to maintain marine aquariums comes to naught are because the average aquarist is almost totally unaware of the enormous ecological problems he is tackling. Successfully keeping a marine aquarium requires a working knowledge of basic principles of physiology, behavior and pollution. This knowledge must consist not only of facts and figures learned from lectures and books, but also of an overall comprehension of essential requirements of his animals and his aquarium. He must know that his animals depend on a healthy aquarium for their own health, and that most things he does to his fish or his aquarium will have some effect that will assure success or failure. He must understand how his aquarium and its fish function together so that when he makes changes he will have some idea of how the entire system might react. If he changes the kinds of lights he is using, for instance, he will want to know not only how this will affect the color of the fish and the attractiveness of the aquarium, but also whether this will change the kinds of algae that are growing within it that in turn can affect the health of his fish.

To plunge into the hysteria of trying to set up and maintain a marine aquarium with less than a good, detailed knowledge of the complex workings of both fish and aquarium is to insure a high percentage of failure. It is a sad waste of both nervous and financial resources of people, but a sadder waste of precious animal life that even today is dwindling and becoming extinct because of the onslaught of the many-pronged ravages of man upon their environment. High mortalities in aquariums are hastening the end of this living beauty that has come to us through trackless time and will revert to nothing unless they are understood, appreciated and cared for.

It is unfortunate, but true, that the average aquarist has to go through years of heartbreak to learn to maintain successfully a marine aquarium. This book, therefore, is dedicated to the task of eliminating the long and expensive tenure needed to develop this ability. It presents sufficient background in marine ecology and an ordered method to guide him in keeping marine fishes in a healthy, satisfying condition. It is hoped and expected that both man and fish will benefit.

Section

I

SALTWATER
AQUARIUMS

1

Setting Up the Aquarium

The following method for setting up an aquarium has proved reliable, and it is recommended that the instructions be followed faithfully even if one has had previous experience. Some variability in materials and procedures is presented to offer latitude for those who might not be able to obtain particular items or who might house an aquarium under varying conditions.

TYPE OF AQUARIUM

The aquarium should be constructed entirely of glass. Although this kind of aquarium is simple, it is recommended that one be purchased rather than made because of special knowledge and techniques that are employed during construction. Glass is not affected by the highly corrosive action of salt water, which is something that always should be kept in mind when working with this medium. An aquarium of at least 30-gallons capacity should be used. Physical and chemical changes occur less rapidly in larger volumes of water; thus, there is more chance for error without disastrous results.

FILTRATION

Subsand, or undergravel filtration, provides a powerful tool for keeping water crystal clear and especially for processing some harmful waste products that otherwise would pollute the aquarium and kill the fish. The basic component is a plastic plate perforated with holes or slits that fits snugly on the bottom of the aquarium. An arrangement of plastic pipes, or airlift, fits into a hole in the corner of the plate, and when an air pump is connected through an air hose, water is drawn from under

Water flows through a subsand or undergravel filter (sand not shown).

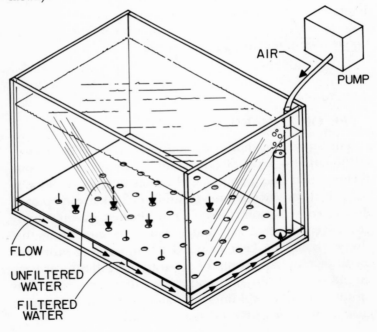

AIR

PUMP

FLOW

UNFILTERED WATER

FILTERED WATER

the plate and leaves with bubbles via the tube. Water is drawn downward through the perforations in the plate to replace that withdrawn from under it. Filter plates should be washed with mild detergent and rinsed well before they are introduced into an aquarium. Since two or more airlifts are employed in most aquariums, a "gang valve" is needed to divide the air between them. The life of the pump will be prolonged by employing a gang valve that has one more outlet than is needed. In this way excess air that creates back pressure on the pump can be bled off by slightly opening the valve after the airlifts are all functioning at the desired rate. The gang valve block should be constructed of plastic and either plastic or brass valve stems are satisfactory.

PROTEIN SKIMMER

Along with the subsand filter, the aquarium must be provided with a protein skimmer (also called a foam dome or electrostatic filter). This indispensable unit acts like ocean waves that produce bubbles in the natural environment. Although it is unknown what part ocean bubbles play in keeping the natural environment clean, it is certain that the protein skimmer plays a large role in performing this function in aquariums. It is true that some marine aquariums do not need this instrument because the aquarist knows how many fish his system can accommodate without waste products accumulating to harmful proportions. However, months are required to achieve this state and then it usually only can be accomplished by an experienced aquarist. For all but a few people, a protein skimmer is essential because it removes the rapid buildup of some harmful materials that cannot

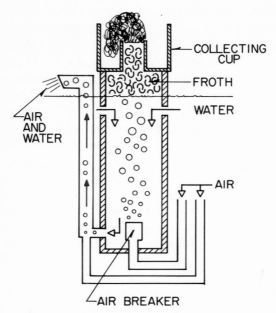

How the protein skimmer operates.

be tolerated for long by fish. When an aquarium is first set up, the skimmer removes materials such as albumins, which, if present at this time when nitrogen is high, would present an even more critical situation for fish. Later, it continues to remove materials that probably accumulate too fast for bacteria to remove, although it may at times have less work to do than in the beginning. One can see indications of skimmer activity within minutes after feeding by an increase in the froth that is formed and removed. The activity slows within minutes or hours as the excess of harmful materials is removed.

The protein skimmer functions by producing a massive column of fine bubbles to which contaminating materials stick. Water from the aquarium flows downward through the bubbles which are rushing upward, and is cleaned. When the water reaches the bottom of the column, it is returned to the aquarium through another tube mounted alongside the central one containing the large mass of bubbles. The bubbles that gather the contaminants expand as they rise and gather in the top in a small chamber. As contaminants continue to gather in the chamber the bubbles there become larger because of a decrease in surface tension. The froth that is so formed puffs upward from the chamber through a tube and collects in a cup which can be emptied when full.

Commercial protein skimmers are available and take much of the uncertainty out of maintaining marine aquariums. About the only maintenance required is the occasional renewal of the air breaker that forms the fine bubbles needed. The need for a new air breaker is evident when bubbles become several diameters larger than when the element is new. Bubble sizes should be judged where they leave the air breaker. Adjustable air breakers should be set so the finest bubbles possible are produced. An occasional cleaning may be needed when sludgelike material becomes thick in the chamber of the skimmer.

FILTERING AIR

It is recommended that the air going into the aquarium be filtered if the latter is situated in a place where cigarette and other fumes are heavy. Most pumps have a filter where the air enters them, but this is mainly for catching dust. There are fumes that will harm fish when brought into the water through the air pump and these can be reduced or eliminated by installing a filter in the air line coming from the pump. These are commercially available and use charcoal and possibly other materials to remove fumes.

BOTTOM MATERIAL

After air tubing is fitted to all the airlifts the filter plates can be covered with a layer of gravel about 1 inch in depth. The relatively large spaces between the particles act as a reservoir from which water is drawn by the subsand filter. A grain size of about one-fourth inch will do a good job. Gravel should be washed in a plastic barrel or other container a few pounds at a time until the wash water is clear, a process sometimes taking 10 or 15 minutes. Granite or quartz gravels are safe to use, but materials such as metallic ores which may give off poisonous compounds are not. After the gravel has been poured, it can be smoothed by hand. Filter plates should be moved away from the sides of the aquarium before pouring or they will show since gravel cannot fall between them and the glass.

Whereas gravel can be composed of hard rock that does not dissolve, sand that is put into a marine aquarium should be composed of a calcareous (calcium) material. Marine sand from coral reefs is an excellent medium because it is composed of fragments of calcareous parts from many kinds of organisms. Crab claws, mollusk and sea urchin shells, and calcareous algae are abundant in many such areas and their grain size and porosity allows them to dissolve readily releasing calcium vital for good health of marine fishes. Some aquarists use a layer of crushed oyster, clam shells or dolomite instead of sand which also seem to do a good job. Such material is more available to aquarists living north of the tropics. Sands composed of naturally rendered parts of marine animals may be available on some northern beaches. Examination under a lens of a low-power magnification will reveal the proportion of calcareous-type grains that are present. Probably it is not advisable to use a sand unless it is at least 80 to 90 percent of calcareous material.

Sand must be thoroughly washed, like gravel, until it is clean. With purely calcareous sand, agitation by hand will leave some cloudiness as the grinding action releases large amounts of calcium. This should not be misinterpreted as "dirty water." When sand is not agitated and water is clean, it is ready for use. About an inch of sand on top of the gravel is sufficient.

WATER

Water of sufficiently good quality for marine aquariums can be obtained from a number of sources. An easy method is to buy a good brand of "synthetic" seawater such as Instant Ocean and mix it according to directions. One of the advantages of this method is that one has little worry about the water being contaminated with polluting materials or organisms harmful to fish. Such water, however, is relatively sterile and must be inoculated with living bacteria.

If one lives in coastal areas where salt water is available, this natural source can be used. However, a number of precautions are advised to prevent the use of undesirable water. It should be collected from offshore areas away from land runoff which may dilute it or introduce pesticides and other pollutants. As a general rule, the farther from shore the water, the more clear it is and free from diluting and polluting materials. Sediment-laden water is to be avoided if possible because of the potential for decay of the suspended particles and because they may carry concentrations of disease-producing organisms as well as noxious materials.

Unless it is obtained far offshore where it is very clear, water should be thoroughly filtered before it is used in aquariums. The best kind of filter for this use is one employing diatomaceous earth as the entrapping agent. The fine-straining action that is created will remove a great many kinds of very small organisms that may cause problems in aquariums. It will remove larger-sized particles to which diseases may adhere and which may themselves foul an aquarium. Filtering a 20-gallon batch of water for one hour at a rate of 150 to 200 gallons per hour will make it crystal clear and reduce numbers of free-living organisms to a degree where they are not an immediate problem. This is not the ultimate answer to disease-free fish, however, as other practices to be outlined must be followed, but this kind of filtration will yield excellent water with which to initially fill the aquarium.

REDUCING SPLASH

One problem in keeping marine aquariums that is not related to water quality (except through evaporation) is bursting bubbles on the surface. They not only leave salt deposits on everything they strike, but also cause salt water to drip down outside the glass. Attention must be given to a means of reducing this problem.

The construction of a splash plate is complicated by the need for proper lighting and aeration. Further details will be found in "Lighting the Aquarium," page 82, but for the moment it should be mentioned that aquariums completely covered with glass or Plexiglas strain out light rays such as ultraviolet which may play a part in maintaining good water quality. If completely covered, exchange of gases at the surface may be altered with changes in water quality eventually following. On the other hand, some kind of covering is necessary because of the splash problem. A compromise has been worked out that permits light to fall directly on the water while retarding the effects of splash and has proved satisfactory, although not perfect. The design also exposes the water directly to the

Construction of a splash plate that reduces effects of bursting bubbles.

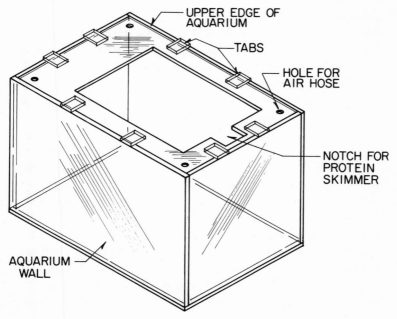

UPPER EDGE OF AQUARIUM

TABS

HOLE FOR AIR HOSE

NOTCH FOR PROTEIN SKIMMER

AQUARIUM WALL

air over it, which at least simulates the natural situation found in the sea.

For aquariums that are divided at the top by a brace, two splash plates must be made. These may be constructed of one-fourth inch thick Plexiglas which snugly fits the inside dimensions of each of the openings resulting from the presence of the brace. Braces often are not set across the middle of the top, so the openings may be of different sizes. An inch and one-half wide splash plate can be constructed that runs around three sides of the opening, but is about 6 inches in width at the end. This provides a platform on which a pump, gang valve or other equipment can be set to hide it from view after the hood is on. Small tabs of Plexiglas are glued to the top of the plate and hang over the sides so that when the plate is set inside the aquarium, they rest on the edge of the glass; thus, the plate hangs inside the aquarium. When drops of water form on this plate as bubbles burst, they may flow to the sides, but fall back into the aquarium instead of running down the outside as happens when a piece of Plexiglas is laid on top. The tabs should not extend past the outside diameter of the aquarium as they will interfere with a hood. Plexiglas can be conveniently cut with a saw and can be glued with ethylene dichloride which forms a rigid molecular bond. Notches can be cut in the Plexiglas (or holes drilled) so that air lines can pass from within the tank without preventing the splash plates from fitting snugly against the glass.

Covering only a narrow strip around the aquarium and part of the end portions does not significantly reduce the total area of water surface that is exposed. The middle portion of the surface remains unobstructed and all light rays reach the water. Since light also shines at an angle, it is likely that the ends of the aquarium also receive unobstructed rays.

AIR PUMPS

The selection of an air pump must be made with due consideration for the devices it will operate. Protein skimmers use a considerable amount of air and also require strong pressure to overcome the back pressure of the air breaker. If no more than two airlifts are operating the subsand filter, it is possible also to operate a protein skimmer from a vibrator pump. However, if four airlifts are used with the skimmer, it may be necessary to use a second pump to operate the latter. When using a second pump a valve bank containing at least three outlets should be used, so one is available for bleeding excess air that otherwise would overdrive the skimmer and cause excessive wear on the pump.

An air pump has two major requirements. It should be powerful and quiet. Pumps that operate on the vibrator principle are usually more quiet than piston types, but they do not deliver as much air. Quiet vibrator types are available, however, that are powerful enough to operate four airlifts without producing sound audible enough to be offensive. It is better to use two such pumps rather than one piston type unless noise and occasional maintenance is not objectionable.

HOODS AND LIGHTS

It is difficult to buy ready-made light fixtures and hoods that will fit all sizes of aquariums. Light banks and hoods apparently are made mostly for freshwater aquariums and are constructed from metals that soon will deteriorate. If the components, i.e., reflectors and sockets, are sprayed with a nontoxic silicone spray in areas where sea-

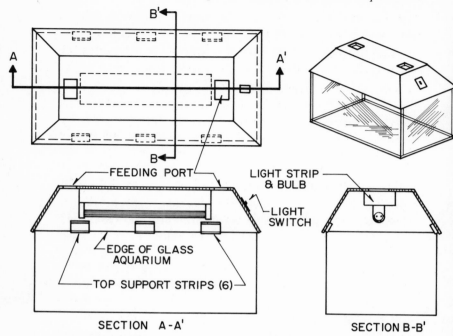

Construction of aquarium hood and light fixture (side, top, end and overall views).

water spray is likely to reach them, it is possible to protect them for a while.

One important function of a hood is to provide a place from which lights can be hung. When maintaining a marine aquarium it is an aid to have a fluorescent light fixture that will accommodate two bulbs. For instance, the use of a long wave ultraviolet bulb seems to have a therapeutic value when fish become sickly. With a two-fixture unit, they can be burned along with other kinds of bulbs so that their purplish glow need not be the only lighting in the aquarium. If constructed properly, a hood also serves to hide pumps and other equipment from view. The construction of the splash plate provides platform space for installing such devices within a hood.

The average aquarium hood requires no more than one 5-by-5 foot piece of plywood one-fourth inch in thickness. The dimensions of the sides and ends will depend on the length and width of the aquarium, but the height should be about 10 or 11 inches above the top of the glass. The parts of the hood can be nailed together to make the construction simpler. All four sides should be canted inward about 10 degrees which gives a sloping, rooflike effect and prevents the hood from appearing like a box. The top of the hood rests on its four sides and is nailed to them. The hood drapes over the sides of the aquarium to produce a tentlike effect. To achieve this, the bottoms of the sides are cut slightly longer than the top dimensions of the aquarium so the hood fits down over it. Strips of wood nailed about one and one-half inches above the bottom of the hood on the inside catch on the rim of the aquarium so that the hood sits on it. This arrangement hides the water line, thus removing this eye-distracting influence.

A fluorescent light strip that accommodates either one or two bulbs is screwed to the inside top of the hood. The leads from the strip are attached to a toggle or other switch that permits turning it on or off from outside the hood. Before the cover is put on the strip, all surfaces including contacts are sprayed with a nontoxic silicone spray that will prevent rust for about a year if applied thoroughly. The small amount of water dripping off these treated surfaces will not harm the fish. The height of the hood reduces the amount of salt deposits or condensation on light fixtures although they should be wiped clean from time to time.

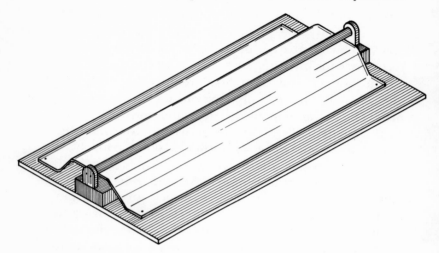

Hanging plastic sheet for protection of electrical fixture.

Another way of protecting hanging electrical fixtures is to hang thin plastic sheeting around them. This can be hung only over the terminals leaving most of the bulb to shine directly on the water. The sheeting merely is tacked to the inside top of the hood and loops downward around the fixture. The "heads" of the tacks should be sprayed with silicone to retard rusting. Plastic sheeting also can be looped from the hood so it passes between the electrical fixture and the bulb to protect the former.

2

Filling the Aquarium

After the water has been filtered it can be poured. Newspapers placed around the aquarium will help to keep the place clean in case water is spilled. Place a large plate or other nonmetal flat object inside the aquarium on the sand and pour the water onto this to break the force. If water is poured directly on the sand, it will dig a large hole disrupting the layering of sand and gravel and forcing sand under the filter plate.

After the aquarium has been filled, it may be somewhat cloudy. However, after the filters begin to function, this fine suspension will gradually disappear in a matter of hours. On the other hand, the aquarium may be clear at first and turn cloudy after three or four days indicating that a large population of microorganisms has developed in response to nutrient material in the water. This will remain for a day or two as the organisms consume all of this material and the water will suddenly become crystal clear and will remain so. These conditions do not always occur, but they are no cause for alarm. If the aquarium has been inoculated heavily with "live" sand the bacterial "bloom" may occur within a day or two.

EARLY CHANGES IN AQUARIUM WATER

When an aquarium is first set up, the most important problem arises from the buildup of nitrogen-containing materials in the water. These result from the activities of bacteria that change animal excretions, leftover food and dead material from one kind of chemical to another. The most toxic of these chemicals is ammonia, which appears early in the series of transformations that involve nitrogen. Ammonia builds up in a new aquarium because the heterotrophic bacteria that produce it multiply faster than those that use it to form nitrite, a less toxic compound. When populations of the former decline and stabilize, species of autotrophic bacteria begin to change ammonia to nitrite on a large scale. As ammonia levels become low, other species of autotrophic bacteria multiply and change nitrite to nitrate, which is less toxic than the former materials. The latter material is transformed by other bacteria into nitrous oxide and free nitrogen, which are not harmful to fish and other aquarium animals in the proportions in which they usually are found. This "nitrogen cycle" operates the same way in the aquarium as it does in the sea. However, the sea is a balanced system in which the great volume of water, its movement, the spacing between animals and other factors continually work together to maintain good water quality. When first set up, an aquarium is not a balanced system and a period of time is required before the nitrogen cycle can become established under conditions that are not identical with those found in the sea. This is the most critical period for animals in an aquarium and it must be approached with knowledge and understanding.

When an aquarium is set up according to the instructions in this book, bacteria and other organisms are pre-

sent in relatively small numbers even though natural seawater and sand may have been used. Growth eventually
will occur because some microorganisms will have sur-
vived the cleanings given the sand and water and some
will be introduced along with fish and their food. Waiting for the proper bacteria to multiply is impractical, for
it may take months and may result in undesirable kinds
of organisms becoming established. The proper bacteria
can be quickly obtained by scraping at least two cupfuls
of sand from the bottom of a healthy, established marine
aquarium and spreading it over the surface of the sand in
the new one. Try to obtain mostly the upper inch of sand
because this is where the necessary bacteria populations
are the most dense. Usually, "dirty" water is transferred
along with the sand. This should not be viewed with
alarm as the material causing the cloudy water is made up
of huge numbers of very small particles to which millions
of bacteria cling. Together with the sand, this detrital
and other material will inoculate the aquarium with
large enough numbers of bacteria so their reproduction
will populate the aquarium with needed numbers within
a matter of a few days or weeks. Although numbers of
some bacteria will continue to change and will not stabilize for several months, inoculation will make it possible
to begin introducing a few fish immediately. Doing this
assures that newly inoculated bacteria will have available the excretions from fishes that enable them to multiply.

Even though the aquarium will be livable for a few fish
at first, it by no means will be stable. The nitrogen-containing materials will increase and decrease in turn in the
aforementioned order until eventually all reach minor
proportions at which time they will not harm fish. The
aquarist can easily get an indication of what is happening
by using a cheap commercially available kit for testing

nitrite. During daily testing he will note how nitrite remains low for the first day or so and then quickly becomes higher. Remember that ammonia is present *before* nitrite sharply increases and is diminishing sometime during the latter's increase. The recommended inoculation possibly results in a quick reaction of bacteria to ammonia so it does not build up or remain in high proportions very long. The nitrite customarily remains in the vicinity of 8 to 10 parts per million for two to four days and then rapidly declines. Healthy reef fishes will survive this level of nitrite for a day or two, but it is not wise to wait too long for the nitrite level to fall. If the level reaches 8 to 10 parts per million and does not drop within twenty-four hours, half the water in the aquarium should be changed. This dilutes the nitrite to a safer level where it probably will remain for a short period of time and then decrease to a point where it is undetectable. At this time, fish are past the dangerous period when first setting up an aquarium.

BALANCE IN AQUARIUM UPKEEP

Since the term "balance" often is used in aquarium keeping, it is appropriate to mention it here. In an older meaning it refers to a state where plants and animals within a completely enclosed freshwater aquarium are living in a healthy condition with each other's waste products being recycled. Such a state is difficult to attain and would be impractical for marine aquariums because, among other things, fish must be fed continually. The most practical concept that concerns us is the balance, equilibrium or stability that the different nitrogen-processing and other bacteria eventually reach. As mentioned previously, this eventually takes a few months to achieve although fish can be put in sooner. Even after this period of time changes continue to take place in aquarium water which make it more stable. Among these are thought to be the inclusion of growth-promoting and inhibiting agents that might affect bacterial as well as fish and invertebrate life. In aquariums that have been set up for many months, fish can die and decay on the bottom (but not within shells) without polluting the water. The reasons for such stability are complex and are not fully understood.

ADJUSTING AIR AND WATER FLOW

Adjusting the rate of airflow to the airlifts requires patience. One way to do this is to close all valves when starting the pump and then open one at a time until all the airlifts are bubbling at about the same rate. Then the valve without an attached hose which bleeds off excess air can be opened slightly to reduce the flow in the airlifts. If one airlift bubbles too slowly, it sometimes is necessary to close the others to let most of the air pressure flow through it. The other lifts then can be restarted and all can be balanced. This procedure of closing valves and restarting may have to be done a number of times with various valves.

The following method of determining adequacy of water flow through the subsand filter is recommended: It is based on measuring the volume of air delivered by an airlift. This can be done by immersing a graduated cylinder (with a scale up to 100 milliliters) in the aquarium until it fills with water. When full, the cylinder is inverted with the base upward while remaining underwater. In this position, it is moved over the stream of bub-

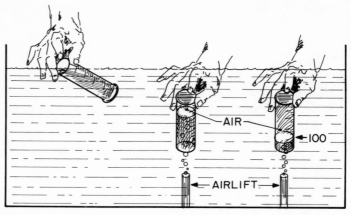

Measurement of water flow through subsand filter by displacement of air.

bles flowing from an airlift so they rise into the cylinder. As the bubbles accumulate in the cylinder, they drive the water out leaving it full of air. The rate of flow is the time it takes to fill the cylinder to a certain point (arbitrarily 100 milliliters) with air. An airlift that delivers this amount of air within ten to fifteen seconds is also delivering enough water through the subsand filter to provide adequate filtration and aeration for the bacteria that are present. It is not necessary to extend an airlift tube to the surface as adequate amounts of water are delivered through shorter tubes. A tube extending halfway to the surface has the advantage of producing more water movement in an aquarium as water is agitated by the rising stream of bubbles.

After air begins flowing, the protein skimmer also must be regulated. After the unit is positioned in the aquarium according to the manufacturer's instructions, the air first is applied through the valve and tubing that feed the air breaker in the large column. It is best to begin regulating the skimmer with this component because the fine pores that cause the bubbles also cause the greatest resistance and once this is overcome and free flow is achieved, the evacuation airlift can be started. The best way to regulate the air entering the large column is to observe the density of the bubbles along its sides. If they are so dense that you cannot see beyond them, sufficient air is being introduced to adequately "wash" the water dropping through them. If bubbles are dense along the sides, they are also dense throughout the column. The collecting chamber at the top of the column should be no more than about a quarter full of bursting bubbles (when they are small and have not yet enlarged) . This leaves most of the chamber where large bubbles and froth can accumulate and eventually spill over the top into the retaining cup where contaminants collect. The flow through the airlift should be regulated so the water returning to the aquarium is flowing about 20 to 30 degrees out from a straight-down position.

If one has used natural seawater and conditioned sand, bubbles probably will grow larger within a day and will begin to spill over as froth in the collecting cup on the top. Within a day, however, they probably will become small again and will burst at their original level as the slight amount of contamination that passed from the sand to the water is removed. Froth may not be formed when using synthetic seawater and with well-washed sand, but it will occur after feeding. Watch the size of the bubbles that are formed near the air breaker when the skimmer is first started so that you have a comparison with those that form later. These bubbles may be large when the skimmer is first started, but should reach the proper small size within 15 to 20 minutes.

PROVIDING HABITAT FOR FISH

It is important to provide a particular kind of habitat for fish that are not acclimated to aquarium life. If not handled properly, newly caught fish may be so badly frightened that chances for their survival will be reduced. Failure to feed, aggression and other social problems are some of the consequences of mishandling. The following steps should be observed with newly caught fish. Fish that are bought probably have been in captivity for a time and may not need these procedures. However, if they act very shy, one can resort to them if necessary.

Proper cover is particularly important in an aquarium because fish cannot escape each other as they can in the sea. Shells, coral or rocks should be introduced and arranged before fish are released. They should be piled up so that a large number of spaces are provided into which fish can disappear from view and remain hidden. A fish that feels secure often will adapt to an aquarium and begin to feed sooner than one that continually is exposed to frightening conditions with no place to hide. Hunger eventually brings most species out of hiding and since they know they can escape, they are more inclined to take an interest in food. It is important to first satisfy their need for protection so fishes' other drives that aid the aquarist can take over.

Any object that is introduced into an aquarium should be scrupulously cleaned. Corals and shells, in particular, should be cleansed of all living or dead matter. Even when they are bought, they should be soaked in fresh water for several days after which rotting material can be detected by smelling the water, the coral or observing material that flies out when hosed with a strong stream of water. This procedure also removes leftover bleach that often is used to remove dead animal material.

Spiral shells are dangerous to keep in aquariums because fish become trapped in the tighter parts of the coils, especially when sick. Whereas a fish will decompose with little effect on the aquarium when it is lying on sand, products from its body will kill all other fish if it decomposes within a shell. Therefore, centers of conch and other spiral shells should be removed to prevent fish from dying there. Spiral shells too small for fish to enter pose no such problem and can be kept in aquariums without alteration.

The amount of cover that is needed mainly depends on the kinds of fish that are introduced. If aggressive species are introduced, they soon will chase other species from cover and even "pin them down" in the upper corners of the aquarium where they may remain until they die. When introducing highly aggressive species such as some damselfish, more cover should be provided. Do not worry about the aesthetic qualities of the aquarium at this time as it is more important to provide fish with their requirements.

3

Catching and Maintaining Marine Fishes

CAPTURE

A fish's fight for survival in an aquarium begins when the collector starts to pursue it in its natural environment. At that moment, the fish is shocked into a state of stress that probably will continue until the time it becomes at ease in its ultimate home away from the sea. If the state of stress continues for a long period of time, and especially if it continues in an environment that is unfavorable to its bodily processes, the animal's chances are slim. Proper handling, even at the time of capture, therefore, is important and must be continued for the rest of the fish's life in captivity.

It is better to catch fish in a way that leaves as little trauma as possible, although frightening them is unavoidable. The more rigorous methods, e.g., using chemicals, can be employed successfully if subsequent handling is good. Different kinds of equipment for catching fish are commercially available, but many collectors prefer to make their own. Commonly used are nets, slurp guns,

Snorkel diver inspects crevice for catchable tropical reef fish. *Courtesy, James W. La Tourrette*

bottles and chemicals that confuse fish. Each has its good and bad points, and the collector would do well to have several kinds of equipment at hand so he can take advantage of the particular conditions he meets. The following methods of capture are commonly employed by collectors:

The use of small hand nets with 8- to 12-inch openings is popular. Square net openings may be somewhat more practical, although uneven features of the bottom at times favor the use of round ones. A clear plastic net with a bag length one and one-half to two times the longest length of the opening is very effective. A bottom made of plastic screen to let water out permits it to be scooped quickly. Plastic material should be a heavy gauge to prevent easy tearing when coral and other objects are accidentally snagged. A handle 1 foot in length is about right for working a hand net. The rim and handle of the net should be made of aluminum or other material which will not deteriorate rapidly when used in salt water. Clear plastic is less easily seen and fish are more likely to enter this type of net. Nets and all other equipment used in salt water should be washed thoroughly after use.

Nets made of mesh sizes as small as one-eighth inch also can be used. This type of net is more easily seen by fish and makes catching them more difficult. Snagging objects is a problem because netting "catches" more easily than plastic and the latter also is more rigid which helps to prevent the problem. Nonetheless, this type of net is effective especially when it is used along with chemicals.

In general, fish are caught with nets by frightening and confusing them. The collector chases them into a hole or attempts to head them off by thrusting the net to the bottom in front of them as they flee. A fish can be routed from its cover by using one hand or a stick and eventually may be successfully herded into a waiting net. Caution should be exercised if one attempts to dislodge a fish from a hole by poking at it with a hand. Moray eels and long-spined poisonous urchins frequent holes and can inflict painful damage to intruding fingers. Some collectors prefer to use two nets since fish often double back and are caught in one or the other. Occasionally, one net is made from visible netting which creates more commotion and heightens the fish's confusion and helps to direct it toward a clear net. Fish often become so confused they will blunder even into the more visible net. When one is trapped, the net is jerked handle first through the water and as the bag swings away it is swung up over the rim, closing the bag.

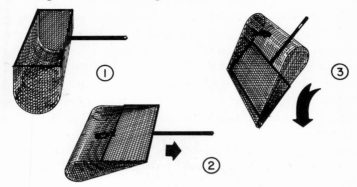

Motions used in closing net after capturing fish.

Extra large nets also can be used effectively especially if collectors work as a team. The rim may be 2 or 3 feet across and the bag 5 to 6 feet in length. Again, a clear net is preferable to one with conspicuous netting. The large net is placed on the bottom and two collectors herd the fish toward the opening. The long length of the bag permits the fish to move far within it without realizing they have been trapped until it is too late to escape. Closing this kind of net is more difficult and may require effort by both collectors. It also is more difficult to work as its size sometimes makes it cumbersome to work with on the bottom.

Hoop nets employed to catch fish can be worked from a boat by the collector. This type has a large diameter rim of 3 or more feet, but the bag of plastic or netting need be only as long as the diameter of the rim. Plastic nets must have a screen bottom to allow passage of water. The net is folded within the rim and the unit is laid flat on the bottom. Three or four lines are attached to the rim and lead to a single line that runs to the surface of the

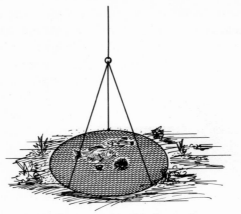

Pull net for capturing fish from a boat.

water. Bait, usually sea urchins which are easy to find in tropical waters, is placed in the center of the net. When fish are actively feeding over the net, it is pulled rapidly all the way to the surface where trapped fish can be removed. Rapidly pulling fish to the surface creates problems, but if fish are handled properly they will probably remain in good health. The hoop net usually is used at depths down to about 30 feet and is effective for capturing fishes such as wrasses that roam the bottom as well as others.

Gallon-sized or smaller bottles can be used to capture fish. Like the hoop net, they are baited and placed near a concentration of fish or perhaps even a particular fish. It is necessary for the collector to remain near enough to cap the bottle when a fish has entered. If the water is shallow enough he can float on the surface with snorkel and mask and dive to seal the bottle. This method depends on the fish becoming confused by the transparent sides of the bottle long enough to permit sealing it.

The slurp gun seems to be popular with some people who claim good results. This device, which basically is a tube and a plunger to pull the water from it, is held in the hand. The snout of the tube is held as close to the fish as possible and the plunger is pulled sharply backward. Water rushes into the end of the tube following the plunger and in so doing pulls the fish into the tube with it. A hand must be placed over the end of the tube to keep the fish from swimming out until it can be forced into a net or bait bucket. Some slurp guns have an arrangement that permits fish to be held in an extra chamber while allowing further use of the instrument.

It takes much practice to use this device effectively. The beginner usually starts out by sucking up sand or other debris in attempts to catch fish near the bottom. Small particles become wedged between the plunger and the barrel rendering the gun difficult or impossible to operate. He will find it no easy task to approach a fish closely enough with the end of the barrel to make the "suction" effective. The proper way to use the gun is to

Slurp gun used to suck fish up from holes.

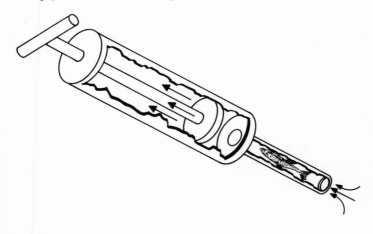

corner a fish in a hole first and hope there is no other exit, or at least that the fish remains near the opening. When the fish holes up, a stream of water is forced out of the gun into the hole. Rather than being forced farther into the hole or against the walls, the fish turns and swims into the current. When the plunger finishes its stroke it is near the opening of the barrel and in position for a fast backward stroke. The fish is not only facing toward the barrel of the gun, but also is swimming toward it so that when the current stops and is immediately replaced by the strong surge it is "sucked" into the barrel. It is recommended that the diameter of the barrel be no more than about 3 inches because of the difficulty in pulling water through the tube.

A method of catching marine tropical fishes that is gaining in popularity is the use of chemical agents that partially anesthetize fish or cause them to lose consciousness. This method is effective, but also is very dangerous if used improperly. A fish's bodily mechanisms are harmed by these poisons, and although it may seem to recover from the effects, it often dies even weeks after being captured and seemingly in good health. Catching fish with chemical agents and successfully keeping them alive and healthy requires definite techniques that begin at the time of pursuit. There is little question that for a fish caught with chemicals to live in an aquarium the water quality must be good. Considerable attention will be devoted to use of chemicals because it is a good way to catch fish if used properly, but also because large numbers of fish are carelessly killed by its use. It is hoped that instruction in the proper use of chemicals will find its way to those who are presently using them incorrectly.

Different collectors use different formulas when mixing the chemical with the necessary ingredient to make it soluble in seawater. The diluting agent itself may be toxic to fishes so that the resulting mixture is a most deadly potion. Undoubtedly, some ratios of the chemical to the diluting agent are more effective and deadly than others, but the important issue in relation to the survival of fish is how any of the mixtures are used.

Use really begins with mixing the chemical. The chemical quinaldine can be used as an example of how to work with such agents in ways that will cause minimum damage to fishes. A mixture of about 1 ounce to 32 ounces of acetone is satisfactory. This amount can be diluted with about one-half pint of seawater. A mixture of about 1 ounce of this material diluted in 10 ounces of ethyl alcohol is said to be less toxic to fish by some collectors. Care should be taken to mix the materials in a place where spilled droplets will not fall on clothes, diving gear, boat decks or other places where the persistent and noxious odor will cause a problem. Great care must be taken to see that drops do not contaminate mouthpieces of diving gear or face masks as the chemical can cause sickness or physical damage to the collector or those around him. Additional care also must be taken to insure that no part of the chemical accidentally enters vessels in which fish are to be held after capture. In small boats where quarters are cramped contamination from chemicals easily can occur, especially if one is unfamiliar with its high potential for dispersal.

The chemical agent can be mixed in a plastic bottle with a spout. A small lead weight in the bottle will prevent it from floating away from the collector and will help to keep the chemicals from settling to the bottom of the container. When in use, the initial mixture is diluted after each squirt from the compressible bottle as seawater runs into it when it regains its shape after pressure from the hand is released. Even though this dilution occurs, many squirts are available that will still effectively confuse the fish. When the material obviously ceases to slow the fish, the bottle can be recharged from a stock solution prepared in advance. When the plastic squirt bottle is filled and recapped, care should be taken to keep it in an out-of-the-way place as even the motion of a boat will cause it to discharge. The opening of the spout of the bottle should always be capped when not in use. A piece of aquarium hose with a knot at one end is convenient for this use.

The proper use of the chemical when catching fish is important. It is squirted into the hole into which a fish has retreated. The safest way is to deliver a one-second squirt and then to "fan" it into the hole gently with a motion of the hand. If the fish is affected by the chemical, it will usually dart around and sometimes shake its head vigorously. Often, it will dart out of the hole and enter another. When this happens, the procedure of squirting should be repeated. A net is held over the opening of the hole or near it after the material has been introduced and often a fish will be snared after two or three squirts. Squirting a larger amount into a hole to chase out a fish should only be done as a last resort. Sometimes this procedure stuns a fish into unconsciousness, which most likely injures it more seriously than when it is only slowed down. Once a fish has left its cover, it should be pursued vigorously and every attempt should be made to capture it in its slightly groggy state rather than using more chemical.

Occasionally, it is necessary to use greater amounts of chemical to offset problems that are encountered. Currents may quickly dilute the chemical making it necessary to use more. When currents are flowing from the hole toward the collector, the chemical will not drift toward the fish. In this case, often it is possible to find another entrance to the hole upcurrent where the chemical will flow toward the fish. Strong fanning with a hand sometimes will blow the chemical into the hole against a weak current; in some instances an arm can be extended cautiously into the hole so the chemical can be closer to the fish. Surge also can cause a problem and the collector must wait until a back surge is traveling toward a hole before releasing the chemical.

The reader is cautioned that use of chemical agents is illegal in some states so attention must be paid to existing laws.

Once a fish has been captured in a net, it must be handled carefully. It should remain on the bottom and not immediately brought to the surface. There are at least two reasons for this. If a fish has been caught by using chemicals, it should be given as long a period of time as possible in flowing water to help it recover. Keeping the

Bait bucket for holding fish underwater after capture.

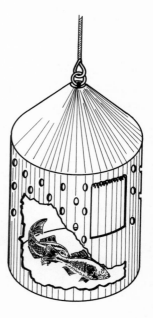

fish on the bottom in a container in which seawater can flush in and out washes away quantities of chemical that might be present on or in the fish and assures a good supply of oxygen at a time when the fish is in great stress and needs it. The other reason for keeping newly caught fish on the bottom is because those with air bladders swell upon being brought to the surface which adds considerably to their already distressed state and may damage them physically. If a fish has recovered before it is brought to the surface, it is not as weak and can withstand better the effects of a swollen air bladder.

Bait buckets commonly used by hook and line fishermen are ideal for holding fish on the bottom. They are provided with hinged doors that spring shut after a fish is introduced and with holes in a number of places so they are continually flushed by currents as they are pulled through the water behind the collector. The lower half of the bucket usually retains water after it is lifted from the sea and the fish are not left flopping while they are transferred to containers on board the boat. A conspicuous yellow polypropylene line attached to a bait bucket will float above it as it rests on the bottom making it easy to locate when the collector has lost it, as often happens when a fish is chased. The line also is used to pull the bucket from one location to another and for hauling it slowly to the surface so that fish have time to decompress (preventing swollen air bladders, protruding eyes and/or internal organs). Some bait buckets have air floats which must be punctured to permit them to sink so they will not float away from the collector.

Care should be exercised in removing the fish from the net and transferring to the bait bucket. Fish often are lost during this maneuver or are damaged. The fish should be herded deep into a corner of the net and carefully grasped, preferably in the cup of the hand. During this procedure, fish often slip past the hand to parts of the net where they might escape. If the collector rises off the bottom, he sometimes can renet an escaping fish since it has to swim some distance downward to reach the bottom. When grasping the fish, care should be taken not to tear mouth parts or fins that might become entangled in netting. Small fish can be held by cupping the hand around them, but larger ones must be grasped by the body. They can be released into the bait bucket by slightly opening the part of the hand that is partially in the door of the bucket into which they will dart when the pressure on them is released. Another and possibly less traumatic method for removing fish is to grasp them in a corner of the net from outside. Holding both gently, the hand, net and fish are pushed through the frame turning it inside out. The fish then is released into the container without having been touched by the hand itself. Fish within the bucket usually hover in the far corner and seldom attempt to swim past a hand presented in the opening.

If possible, raising fish to the surface should be done slowly so those with an air bladder will swell less as they approach the surface. From depths of a hundred or more feet an air bladder may swell to such proportions that it is forced out of a fish's mouth. In shallow waters where most collecting is done, however, swelling of this organ is visible as a swollen belly. Swelling can damage the fish internally and if great enough can cause it to float helplessly to the surface where it struggles in vain to return to the bottom of the vessel in which it is kept. As a rule, large fish swell to larger proportions than smaller ones and the problem of floating is more severe.

The depth at which fish are caught determines the length of time it takes to raise them to the surface. In depths up to 30 or 40 feet, they can first be raised 5 or 10 feet off the bottom and the line tied off on the boat for fifteen or twenty minutes. The next haul can raise them to within 10 feet of the surface where they again can be held for half an hour. After this they can be hauled into the boat and placed in holding containers. From greater depths, fish can be hauled to half the distance to the surface for the first stop.

The length of time it should take to raise fish to the surface is arbitrary. Some collectors haul them to the surface immediately although only a few feet each minute. To thoroughly decompress fish takes a long time, which most people feel they cannot afford to spend. If at all possible, they should be held some 10 feet under the surface for as long as practical. There is a great deal of variability with some species swelling more than others and some not swelling at all.

Raising fish with a line tied to the boat also can cause problems. When the surface is rough the suspended bait bucket snaps violently at the end of its rope. Fish are buffeted around within the vessel and, besides being even more frightened, may be injured against the sides. Under these conditions it is probably better to raise them immediately to the surface and bring them into the boat. This condition can be avoided by placing a float on the bucket so it is suspended above the bottom like an underwater buoy. Since the buoyed bucket floats underwater, the collector must enter the water to adjust the line and permit it to float successively closer to the surface. This is a laborious procedure, but is safer for the fish.

It is important to hold fish properly when they are brought aboard a boat. Everything possible must be done to make these delicate animals feel at home. There is good reason for taking elaborate procedures to fulfill this objective. When fish are under stress, their bodily or physiological activity rates are very high. This high rate appears to damage fish physically and later can lead to death if conditions in the aquarium are not optimum. Poor procedures, such as inadequate aeration, bouncing around in a boat and leaving the vessel containing the fish in the sun where the water heats up can kill them before they are ever brought to shore.

A large container should be used to hold fish on a boat until they can be placed in an aquarium. A 20-gallon plastic garbage can with a lid will fulfill this purpose. This container preferably should be filled with seawater or at least with freshwater and aerated for weeks before fish are kept in it to leach out undesirable chemicals from the plastic. Cans made of polyethylene are very good, although they too should be "cured" and also aerated for weeks. Uncolored plastic is less likely to contain harmful materials, but this is not necessarily always the case. Cans that smell strongly may be difficult to cure or leach.

Before newly caught fish are placed in the container, the collector should fill the bottom with rocks he picks from the bottom before he begins collecting or preferably with rocks he has brought from home. Ideal rocks are those with shallow cavities and crevices or with a concave surface under which fish can hide. Rocks, shells, etc., used for this purpose should be free of living marine growth. Shells and rocks with deep holes should be avoided because fish can become lodged within and may die there. It is better to have at least two layers of rocks to give fish room to hide, to get away from each other and to reduce sloshing of water when the boat rolls and later when the container is moved. Before rocks, etc., are put into the container, they should be thrashed vigorously through the water to wash out loose particles and silt. When they are placed in the container, try to wedge them so rolling and pitching will not cause them to shift position and injure or crush fish hiding under them. Most species will immediately hide among the rocks in the container and become quiescent. Under these conditions, fish become calmer and even have been observed feeding on overgrown rocks in their first hours of captivity.

Problems with aggression often arise in containers in which fish are being held shortly after capture. Aggressive species chase others out of rocks unless they can find narrow crevices into which they can escape. Individuals of some species such as rock beauties and some damselfish should be kept in separate containers as they may damage or kill others of the same species. Adequate water should be kept in the container so that fishes chased out of rocks can remain above them. This water usually will be utilized by timid species as an area of escape in a varied catch.

After fish are in the container, it should be covered by a lid and kept in the shade. If continuous aeration is not available, an adequate supply of oxygen can be furnished by scooping up the water with a cup or bucket and pouring it down the sides into the container. Flowing water spreads out along the sides and is efficient in picking up oxygen. Doing this several minutes each half to three quarters of an hour is adequate. A cheap, battery-operated air pump and air stone is a good investment that will supply water in a container with sufficient amounts of oxygen to keep fish in good condition. It is important to bucket out as much water as possible a few times before refilling the container for the trip to shore, since fish must remain in this water until they are put into an aquarium. Under no circumstances should fish be kept in a bait-well through which water flows from outside the boat. Water close to land may be polluted and may be chemically and physically different from that in which the fish had been living. The sudden change in water quality may kill or damage them.

When fish are brought to shore, and if they will not be

in transit for more than two or three hours, some of the water in their container can be removed to lighten the load. When this is done, one should bear in mind that reduced amounts of water will become loaded with waste products from both fish and any growth that is present in the container, or on the rocks, and the oxygen will be depleted faster. While little can be done about waste products at this point, oxygen can and should be replenished as previously outlined. Ordinarily, fish will hold well under these conditions, but the less time they have to withstand them, the better. It is better to keep the original amount of water to avoid problems with aggression, quick temperature changes and buildup of products that foul the water. Deeper water also reduces sloshing which can injure fish by banging them against rocks and the sides of the container and by heightening their excited state. Precautions must be taken to keep the water temperature from changing too fast, especially when a great difference exists as often occurs even in subtropical areas. If fish are transported at night, the container should be lighted to enable them to see and to avoid being thrown against the rocks by whatever water motion that occurs.

The collector must be very careful when collecting on coral reefs. The usual tendency when chasing a fish is to forget about everything else. Strenuous effort is needed to push about the ocean floor with hands, legs, elbows, and the like. Inevitably a person brushes against objects growing there, often with painful consequences. Not only is there the danger of dashing parts of one's body into sea urchins which leave broken spines embedded in flesh, but there also is an ever-present possibility of contacting poisonous forms of marine growths. Prominent among these are the featherlike branches of hydroids, red stinging sponges and the flat blades of yellow fire coral. The latter also coats the surfaces of branching gorgonians which often are brushed by divers. Moray eels also are present on coral reefs and may bite viciously. They mostly lurk in holes so hands should never be thrust blindly into such places.

INTRODUCING WILD FISH TO THE AQUARIUM

Introducing newly caught fish into an aquarium is a critical operation. Differences must be assumed to be great between chemical and physical composition of the water in which fish were caught and transported and that into which they will be introduced. It is possible that a healthy aquarium with good water quality will have conditions not too different from those found in the sea, but this should never be assumed.

The essence of transferring fish to their new home is to do it gradually. This gives a fish a chance to become physiologically accustomed to differences that exist. Variations in hydrogen-ion concentration (pH), temperature, nitrogen content and other factors are compounded to set up a physiological jolt from which a fish might eventually die. The change from a free to a captive existence is more severe than moving a fish from one healthy aquarium to another after it is acclimated to life in captivity. Not only is the water in the sea different, but it too changes considerably in composition as a fish remains in it for a number of hours while it is being transported. The degree of a fish's stress also undoubtedly builds up along with waste products. Nonetheless, in spite of these changes, it is important not to change the fish's water until it is being introduced into the aquarium.

The first step is to lower the water level in the container in which the fish has been transported if this was not done previously. This procedure keeps to a minimum the water that must be taken from the aquarium to dilute that in which the fish are held. An amount of water equal to about one-fourth of the water in which the fish is being held should be removed from the aquarium into which it is to be transferred. This should be poured into the container and thoroughly mixed with the water already there. Constant aeration provided during this acclimation procedure helps keep pace with the fish's high rate of respiration and mixes newly introduced water. After about one-half hour the same amount of water again is poured into the container with the fish. This is a somewhat milder dilution than the first because the volume of water in the container was increased by the first dilution. The original amount of water should be added each half hour until four or five additions have been made. One-half hour after the last addition, the fish are ready to be placed in the aquarium having had sufficient time to acclimate to temperature and other important conditions.

The next procedure is to sterilize the surface of the fish. This is done to reduce disease-causing organisms that reside on the gills and other surfaces of the fish. Although this procedure imposes an added burden on the fish because of the toxicity of many sterilants, it is necessary and is not considered debilitating if carried out carefully. The chance of introducing disease into an aquarium must be reduced as much as possible.

Various chemical agents in the proper proportions can be used to sterilize fish. The author's experience with potassium permanganate has been successful and will illustrate the procedure, although other materials will demand other amounts and times that fish may be exposed to them.

An amount of potassium permanganate crystals or fragment of a pill about the size of a small pin head should be dissolved in about four cups of tap water. Distilled water can be used, but is not considered necessary because fish will be in it only a short time and the treatment is undoubtedly more rigorous than even poor tap water would provide. Make sure all the chemical is dissolved before proceeding.

Before preparing to sterilize, one should slowly remove the rocks from the container in which fish are being held so they can easily be caught. Water can be bailed out gently making it easier to catch fish in the small amount that is left. It is better to introduce fish into an aquarium under reduced illumination which helps reduce the shock they experience. Catching fish and transferring them to the solution may be done with bare hands, but there is more likelihood of dropping them. On the other hand, they often become tangled in a net and the resulting struggle to free them may end in a damaged fish. This probably is the best method, however, since the fish can be dipped while remaining in the net and then can be lifted to the aquarium where it is freed. Transfer should take place with both the container of fish and the vessel with the chemical close together. Preferably, one container should be held over the other so the fish will fall into it if it wriggles free. One fish should be sterilized at a time which helps prevent dropping them and allows one to regulate the time a fish remains in the solution.

Fish smaller than about 1 inch should be released in the solution and allowed to remain there only about twenty or thirty seconds. They should be removed immediately after that time and placed in the aquarium.

Larger fish can be left in the solution for 45 seconds. Experience has shown that although fish can tolerate the solution for longer periods of time, they do not develop disease if the above timing is followed. The vessel in which fish are being sterilized should be covered, since they often will attempt to jump out. A piece of writing paper should be kept handy in the event that fish do jump so that they can be easily scooped up and returned to the solution or the aquarium. It is difficult to pick up a fish from a smooth surface with bare hands. The aquarist should not be shocked if fish he puts into a solution of potassium permanganate immediately become stiff and lie on the bottom of the vessel with their fins rigidly spread. Some species seem to go into a state of shock after a few seconds in this solution and appear to be dead. They fully revive, however, when placed in the aquarium after the treatment.

4

Care of Newly
Introduced Fish

When unacclimated fish are introduced into an aquarium, they react in different ways. If sufficient cover is present, many quickly hide whereas others may remain exposed to view at the bases of objects and some even may swim against the glass for a while. Eventually, those that do not at first take cover begin to do so and by the morning after release, most are hiding within the cover where they remain for varying periods of time. At which time they begin to actively swim around depends on many factors.

If no old residents are in the aquarium, the first fish to leave cover may be those that are driven out by more aggressive species. To reduce this problem keep the illumination in the aquarium dim. Activity is sharply reduced with decreasing illumination especially in wild fish. When fish are handled correctly—including darkening the aquarium—they are usually calm though wary the next morning. By this time those that have left their cover do not dash wildly, having had some time to adjust to their situation.

It is desirable to have some species of damselfish in a

new aquarium. Many species are only moderately aggressive and quickly become active although they may stay
close to cover on the bottom. Being very active, damselfish soon begin feeding, often on the day they are introduced. This activity is a help to other fish because it helps
them overcome their shyness and begin to leave shelter
and feed.

If a particular fish is attacked continually and remains
in one corner, it should be removed immediately and put
in another aquarium, unless one separates it from its
adversary by a partition made of some nontoxic material
such as glass. This may not solve the problem since it may
appear again when the partition is removed. However, an
individual sometimes is able to "hold its own" if it has
time to adjust to the aquarium without being harassed as
soon as it is introduced. It is desirable to have a small
holding aquarium available as it can be used for isolating
sick fish or ones that are consistently being attacked by
others. A certain amount of aggression is desirable
because it keeps fish active and alert and probably reduces
physiological problems due to sluggishness.

Although feeding will be dealt with in more detail
later, it is necessary to say a few words about it here. If
food is presented properly, fish will begin to feed sooner.
A fist-sized rubber syringe with a spout should be used to
squirt the food gently down to fish as they usually are too
shy to come out and eat it. Although hunger eventually
brings them out, it may take weeks before some will feed,
if ever. When relatively large amounts of food drift down
to them, however, they soon begin to pick at it and
sooner or later one or more will begin to feed vigorously
and the others quickly follow. Using the syringe allows
one to place food where it is known that particular fish
are hiding. Merely dumping the food causes it to disperse
more widely and often it does not drift into the necessary

areas of the aquarium. This method introduces more food into the aquarium than will be eaten and increases the danger of fouling, or pollution. However, the three or four days that may be needed to get fish feeding will not cause a problem in a new aquarium as outlined here and after this period of time it will be cleaned. With wild fish it is best for the aquarist to remain out of sight after introducing food so fish will come out to feed more readily. Once they start feeding he can stand quietly in view and eventually begin to be less cautious as the fish become less fearful.

When most fish reach the stage where they feed immediately when food is presented, excess rocks and other cover can be removed. This should be done as quietly as possible since fish often become excited and may injure themselves as they dart around. Care should be taken that no rocks are dislodged as they may injure fish as they fall or change position. Since fish at this time are already partially acclimated they soon will become accustomed to the reduction in cover. Some fish, however, may be much wilder than others (e.g., blue chromis and jawfish) and may jump out. Be prepared to scoop them up with a piece of stiff writing paper or similar material.

Within the next two or three days, half of the coral and other cover should be removed from one end of the aquarium so that fish still have cover in which to hide in the remaining half. Gently herd fish away from the bare end of the aquarium with one hand. Sweep a fine mesh net (with pin-head-sized holes or less) back and forth through the water to entrap the large particles of uneaten food and other debris. The action of the net will cause material on the bottom to swirl up where it can be caught. After straining out most of the particles, place the rocks back into the end of the aquarium from which they were removed and then take out those from the other end. Wash the cover in fresh water to remove particles before returning it to the aquarium.

After as many large particles as possible have been removed, a filter should be installed to remove the fine ones. The filter can be an "outside" type that hangs on the side of the aquarium and is powered by a small electric pump. These filters usually siphon water from the aquarium into a container from which it is pumped back after passing through a filtering material such as Orlon, wool or sand. The finer the filtering material, the finer the particles that will be removed. A diatom filter for cleaning the water also can be used. This is an excellent filter because it not only removes small particulate contaminants but also disease-producing organisms that are less likely to cause trouble if they are present in reduced numbers.

Whenever removing cover, caution should be exercised that fish are not hiding in rocks, shells or other cover. It is easy to unknowingly remove fish in this way and to set them aside or immerse them in a cleaning solution or fresh water. This can be avoided if the aquarist keeps track of the number of fish he has and counts them as he removes cover. A good policy is to first remove all objects without holes where fish can hide. Attention then can be focused on the objects that remain since they are the ones most likely to retain fish. The longer fish are held in aquariums the more inclined they are to flee from cover when it is disturbed, but exceptions sometimes occur.

Fish are often difficult to dislodge from cracks or holes. The object in which they are hiding should not be shaken as they will flop around inside and be injured. A good way to remove them after they have been located in a particular object is to slowly draw it out of the water allowing the fish time to swim down as the water level falls within. Often, they will swim downward and as the

Juvenile blue angelfish picks at a potential source of food on a branching gorgonian. *Courtesy, William M. Stephens*

object clears the water the fish will dash to the bottom. It may be necessary to do this several times and to turn the object over with various outlets facing the bottom before the fish will come out. With experience, one automatically notices which fish remain within cover and withdraws the suspected hideout from the water with care. If a fish cannot be removed without shaking, the object should be left in the aquarium. Placing the object in a bucket of water from the aquarium is of little use as a fish so frightened may remain within for a long period of time.

INITIAL LIGHTING

During the period when aquariums are first set up, fish probably are more susceptible to infection because of their weakened condition after capture, because of possible instability in the aquarium at this time and because they are not adjusted to conditions even though the aquarium may be stable. Occasionally, fish are scraped and cut and are even more disease prone. Proper lighting at this time can help fish recover and adjust to life in captivity.

During the first three or four days of captivity, fish should be illuminated with long-wave ultraviolet light. Although it is still questionable whether fish are directly affected or whether conditions within the aquarium become more favorable, experience has shown that this kind of light has a therapeutic effect. Wounds tend to heal and diseases do not appear as frequently when this type of lighting is used. At least one bulb should be used to illuminate the aquarium and if a two-bulb unit has been installed, the other also can be used for this purpose. Apply this illumination throughout the day, but extinguish it at night. This light is rather dim, which also is good for the fish at this stage of acclimation. Ultraviolet bulbs are available in varying lengths, the 4-foot length being designated F40BL and the 2-foot, F20BL. It may or may not be necessary to use two ultraviolet bulbs. If only one bulb of a two-bulb unit is used, it may be necessary to block off the other bulb as some units will not work unless both are lit. This can be done by wrapping aluminum foil around the bulb to prevent light from leaving it.

5

Maintaining
the Aquarium

During the years over which these procedures were developed, it became apparent that five major factors could be combined to insure successfully keeping marine fishes in closed systems, or aquariums. Two of these involve the use of a subsand filter and protein skimmer. Another is establishing the proper kinds of bacteria primarily in the sand. A fourth involves how well fish are treated until and shortly after they enter the aquarium. The first four have been discussed and fish treated and held in these ways will have an excellent chance for survival. This is because both their condition and the water quality will be good. The final factor that will insure continuing good water quality and health is how well the aquarium is maintained subsequently.

Good water quality allows fish to recover after they are introduced into an aquarium and keeps them healthy so that only minor problems with disease and other ill health are encountered. This almost eliminates the need for tampering with water quality by introducing chemicals that may control disease, but also cause changes that often lead to long-term complications and eventual loss of fish.

Fish release solid and liquid wastes and their food introduces both decomposition products and other contamination resulting from materials lost into the liquid when it was prepared. If a good population of the proper kinds of bacteria build up in the sand and on other objects in the aquarium, many of these materials are chemically changed and do not accumulate in amounts that are harmful to fish. If there is a buildup of algae, even more materials are changed into forms that do not appreciably harm fish. However, some materials do not succumb to these natural treatments and build up to levels that pollute the aquarium environment and lead to the death of fish in complex ways. They may aid the buildup of numbers of organisms that are directly harmful to fish or interfere with their health simply because they are so numerous and perhaps change the chemistry of the water. Waste from fish and their food sets in motion changes in the aquarium that in turn weaken the fish's health. In this condition, fish are not as tolerant to changes in temperature, salinity and water chemistry, and are more susceptible to disease. This is a typical way in which ecological factors in a closed system work together to produce changes in the environment and the animals that live therein.

The challenge to the aquarist is to understand what changes to expect, how they come about, which are good or bad and what to do about them. The aquarist is an ecologist in his own right and will not succeed until he understands and can manipulate the many factors that determine the health of his aquarium and its fish. One of the most important of these factors is the food and feeding of fish.

FOOD AND FEEDING—REGULATING AMOUNT OF FOOD

Among the factors that complicate feeding are tastes of individual species, size of individual fish and the problem of polluting the aquarium with uneaten food. Ways of dealing with these problems will be given, but the aquarist must watch closely, especially at first, to see what happens to the food he gives his fish. The proper amount of food depends on how much remains after feeding once fish are eating well. The amount that falls to the bottom during feeding should be noted, but bear in mind that fish may continue to search for food sometime after all of it has been introduced. As a part of watching for potential food pollution, the aquarist should gently stir the bottom every few days to see how much uneaten food is swept up into the water. This can be done by squirting water through a long glass tube with a fist-sized rubber syringe, which eliminates the need for completely removing the hood and thrusting a hand into the water. If a feeding hole has been cut in the hood, it need not even be tilted if the tube is long enough to reach the water. The tube also is useful for squirting water into shells, coral and other cover, thus helping in the removal of food particles that lodge in tight spaces. After becoming familiar with the proper amount of food, this practice need be done only infrequently. Feeding the proper amount of food helps a great deal in preventing pollution.

The size of food particles that are given to fish is an important aspect of antipollution procedures. If food particles are too large or too small, they will not be eaten and will collect on the bottom. In general, large fish select large particles and small fish small particles of food.

Since foods contain an assortment of particle sizes, having different-sized fishes in an aquarium helps to remove many food particles. When feeding, watch the fish and determine the size range of the food particles they take so this factor can be taken into consideration when food is purchased or prepared at home.

FOOD AND FEEDING—KINDS OF FOOD

Although tropical reef fishes eat many different kinds of food in the wild, many of them will eat shrimp when in captivity. Even though they may eat this food well, they should be provided with a supplemented diet to make sure they receive all their nutritional requirements. The aquarist can buy uncooked shrimp, reduce it to the particle size he wishes and can supplement it with commercial foods that will meet the needs of most species. The following formula will keep most species in good health, and proportions can be varied depending on how well fish feed on the various components.

It is cumbersome to mix food each time fish are to be fed. Therefore, preparing a large amount and freezing it saves much time and trouble. If larger carnivorous species are to be fed, the shrimp can be chopped into pieces as large as they will take and then frozen. This is a simpler situation than most aquarists face who have smaller fish. These require more finely chopped particles that take considerable time to prepare by hand. This problem can be overcome by chopping the shrimp in a blender. However, if this is not done correctly, a mush that is too fine will be produced. Therefore, shrimp should be chopped in a blender that has been frozen. The blender (except for the motor) should be placed in a freezer prior to chopping the shrimp. The latter also must remain frozen until chopping begins; otherwise they will warm the jar and mush will result. Chop only a few shrimp at first until familiar with the particle sizes that are best for the fish. When this is determined, large batches can be made and particle size can be adjusted.

After the shrimp is chopped, it should be put into a container and rinsed in fresh water. When it is swirled around and then placed aside for a minute the heavier particles to be retained sink to the bottom first. When they have settled, the liquid which contains many small particles is poured off and more water is added. After this has settled, the water again is poured off and the chopped shrimp is set aside. Whole, frozen brine shrimp now is prepared as an additive. Many fish relish this food, which is very nutritious. A frozen cake of this commercially available food can be broken or cut into a piece that approximately covers the bottom of a shallow aluminum or other container. The chopped shrimp can be poured over this to about the same thickness as the layer of brine shrimp and the container and contents then can be frozen. The brine shrimp is not washed as is the chopped variety because it appears to lose a lot of the important food materials which comprise it.

After the shrimp is frozen in the container, it can be broken up and stored in a freezer in a plastic bag. When feeding, the proper amount is taken out of the freezer and placed in a little water to thaw. It then can be fed to the fish. Food should not be put into the aquarium in the form of an ice cake as it thaws slowly and may remain floating in an inedible chunk. Introducing food in a chunk also may prevent some fish from getting their share as larger fish will feed on it until it is completely consumed.

It is important to wash the food as indicated. When

shrimp or other organisms are chopped a great amount of cellular fluid is released (the aquarium can tolerate the amount introduced with the unwashed brine shrimp). This liquid material cannot be eaten by fishes. However, it is rich in nutrient material and when it enters the aquarium it acts as a fertilizer, which quickly aids growth of bacteria and other organisms that can harm fish either directly or indirectly through their own waste products. Although the filtration devices provided will remove some of these materials, concentrations should be kept as low as possible as time is required for their removal, and the more that are present, the sooner pollution will occur. Lightly washing commercially available foods helps to remove fragments of organisms and other undesirable materials that might have been included when preparing food, but some of the food value will be lost.

A good dried food can be included with the above diet. These foods (as indicated on the labels) provide quite a varied diet which may include such items as crab, fish, mussel, lobster, seaweed and many other organisms. Seaweed, or algae, forms part of the diet of many reef fishes and should be included in the diet of fish in captivity. Dried food with a wide number of dietary items actually is sufficient to meet all the requirements of most marine fishes.

If all fish in an aquarium eat enough dried food to remain healthy, it is the simplest way to feed them. However, a lot of the dried food that is fed consists of flakes that are too small to be eaten and fish often "mouth" even the larger flakes and then spit them out in small pieces that also are not eaten. The amount of this material necessary to keep fish nourished will introduce a large amount of uneaten food. All of this material collects on the bottom and contributes to a potential for pollution. A lot of very small fish in an aquarium will eat more of the finer material and help the situation if dried food is used extensively. However, for an aquarium containing fishes an inch and a half or more in length, it is recommended that dried food of the flake type should be used as a supplement.

Many kinds of foods suitable for reef fishes are available commercially. The aquarist can try such foods as tubifex worms and daphnia along with the regular diet to see how the fish respond to them. If he wishes, he can shift the diet to favor some of these foods, being careful to see that they obtain other foods to round out the diet. Such foods usually have to be fed for some days before fish will eat them.

Care should be taken to prevent fish from becoming conditioned to only one kind of food. This might occur in spite of precautions taken and some species will only eat particular kinds of food anyway. In general, fish will accept a variety of foods if exposed to them properly around the time they first feed in an aquarium. At this time, fish will sample different foods and will come to accept a variety of them. If they are fed on only one kind for several weeks, however, they may not accept others. This prevents giving them a varied diet and also obligates the aquarist to obtain a particular kind of food which occasionally may be unavailable.

If fish tend to pick out a certain kind of food from the variety that is offered to them simultaneously, attempts should be made to try to get them to accept something different. This sometimes can be done by feeding a heavier proportion of the food that one wishes them to become accustomed to and very little of that on which they usually feed. Another method is to feed them a little of the unacceptable food before the usual course is offered. When they are hungry and expecting one kind of food, some species will accept another. A little food also stimulates competition and fish will grab it quickly with less discrimination before others can get it. Commercial "appetite stimulators" are available and can be tried if repeated efforts to feed fish are not successful.

Fish can be fed only once each day and will remain in good condition without losing weight. When they are first introduced to the aquarium, however, they should be fed several times each day until feeding well. Observations should be made to see that all fish are feeding and that some of the aggressive ones are not getting it all. If this is occurring, food can be dispersed in a cup of water and then introduced. In this way, it quickly disperses in the aquarium giving most of the fish a chance to get some. Squirting the food into the aquarium with the syringe and glass tube previously mentioned is a good way to scatter food as it can be aimed at different locations without taking off the hood. Food applied in these two ways also is forced to the bottom where more timid species that are reluctant to leave cover can get it. Over time, however, most species gradually become more accustomed to life in captivity and actively compete with each other for food out in the open.

If many food particles are too large or small and are not eaten, chopping time should be lengthened or shortened accordingly to produce a size range that will be as completely eaten as possible. The feeding habits of each fish in the aquarium will become familiar and this will aid in fixing the proper proportions of ingredients so some species are not underfed. Some particles will remain on the surface and eventually some fishes may feed on them. Particles on the surface usually are not a problem, but they can be removed with a net if they remain for a day. Areas of accumulation in corners, at the bases of objects and within shells and coral should be noted and this buildup withdrawn with the syringe arrangement. If there are corals or other cover with narrow crevices in the aquarium, try to feed to one side of them as some of the food will fall into these hard-to-clean places. Remember that with the syringe and tube food can be squirted out of tight places so fish can get it.

PLANT GROWTH IN THE AQUARIUM

The ecology of a marine aquarium, although similar to the natural environment in many ways, nonetheless is different in many others. In nature, as we will see, the amount of water is very large in relation to the thin veneer of rocks, coral, sand and mud that carpets the bottom. Therefore, waste products are greatly diluted by the water and are also removed by the huge numbers of animals and plants that live on the bottom and in the water. However, this situation does not exist in an aquarium. There is far less water in relation to the fishes as well as to the large numbers of bacteria and other microscopic plants that live on the sides, bottom and many surfaces presented by cover such as shells, coral, rocks and especially the sand. All these plants, fish and food that is introduced produce large amounts of waste materials that the water cannot carry away and that are too much for the microscopic life to utilize quickly. Getting rid of waste products in an aquarium becomes a problem of keeping down the amounts that are produced by limiting primarily the numbers of animals and their food and by introducing filters that both substitute for natural processes and aid those that still occur in an aquarium. Some of these "musts" for aquarium keeping have been dealt with under "Setting Up the Aquarium" and "Food and Feeding" and others will appear later.

One of the ecological principles that apply to the

aquarium as well as to the natural environment is "succession." In the sea, as on land, different kinds of plants and animals "succeed" or replace each other. This particularly is noticeable when a new living area occurs. When the piling for a pier, for instance, is placed in the water or a rock slide plunges into the sea, or a storm scours rocks clean, living areas unpopulated by animals or plants are created and succession begins.

First come microscopic plants and animals in that order and then come larger animals that eat them or take up residence there. As time proceeds, different kinds of life replace each other so that if one observes a piling or other living space over a period of time, one will see that the animals and plants that were formerly there eventually were replaced by others. In the natural environment, and especially on a coral reef, there are many kinds of animals and plants available for this succession and a small area may harbor a wide assortment of individuals.

Succession also occurs in a marine aquarium and the aquarist will have to deal with it. Except for an initial cloudiness that may develop after a day or two and then vanish, little change may be visible for two or three weeks. The time before growth is noticed is variable and is related to a number of factors. If sand and/or water is used that contains large numbers of living microorganisms, growth on the sides, bottom or cover may be noticed soon. If relatively sterile water and sand are used, microorganisms will appear much later since they must build up large numbers from the few that will be introduced along with fish.

After a week or so and before visible growth appears, one can run a hand over the sides of the aquarium and tubes which may feel slimy. This is caused by a layer of bacteria that are probably the first abundant inhabitants of the aquarium. These first species of bacteria may not be necessary for maintaining a healthy aquarium, but their presence as a first step in establishing algal growths is generally acknowledged.

At the time this is occurring, the numbers of nitrogen-processing bacteria are increasing mostly on the sand grains. As water percolates through the sand, these organisms change harmful nitrogen compounds to less harmful ones just as they do in the sea, as we already have seen. Others that coat the corals, rocks, air pipes and airlifts also share in this process that is important in maintaining a healthy aquarium.

Several weeks after the aquarium is set up patches of color may begin to appear at various locations. These are usually brown, green, red or blue green, and their presence heralds a new era in the aquarium. They signal a number of changes that influence the health of the aquarium and the fish. These populations of diatoms, algae and/or bacteria utilize some of the waste products (e.g., nitrates and carbon dioxide) in the water and contribute to good water quality. Some fish also feed on them, which is a valuable supplement to their diets, if not a major item for some species. The presence of these organisms creates a problem since glass must be kept free of them for visibility. Their presence is a welcome sight, however, because good water quality is becoming established when they appear.

Complex ecological factors govern the kind of algae and other growths that occur. The kind of light that is used is one of the most important. Some brownish diatom coatings are favored by low, natural light coming through doorways or windows as well as by some of the fluorescent bulbs used to light the interiors of homes and offices. Higher intensity natural light penetrating aquariums placed near windows promote the growth of green algae whereas some blue-green algae may grow in high or low light. The use of bulbs that are manufactured specifically to grow plants are commonly used to achieve rapid algal growths by some aquarists. As it often turns out, the aquarium probably will have several kinds of plants growing within it, some more numerous than others. Usually, one species eventually will take over most of the surfaces. The surfaces of objects that face the source of light usually have the heaviest coating of plants and are the first places where they occur. Shadowed areas within the aquarium may contain species of plants that thrive better on the lower light found there.

As algae spread and become more abundant, they use nitrates, ammonia, CO_2 and other materials that are produced. Getting rid of excess nitrate is probably beneficial to fish, although it generally is thought that these materials are not particularly harmful. As succession proceeds, however, the algae that die may release pigments that eventually give the water a yellowish or brownish tint. This easily is eliminated within a day by placing commercially available capsules of activated charcoal over airlifts so the water flows through them or using a filter containing this material.

Problems with fish at times may be related to algal blooms. During that time when it seems that some algae "take over" an aquarium, fish sometimes become restless and swim rapidly around and up and down the sides of the aquarium. They also may rub their gill covers against coral or other objects indicating their gills are irritated. It is thought by some that this is caused by large concentrations of microscopic spores that swim from algae as it reproduces rapidly during a bloom and which cling to and irritate fish's gills. There does not seem to be any proof that this is the cause of the problem, but it seems logical in view of the circumstances. There are other things that cause gill irritation (see page 99), but its possible relationship with algae also is noteworthy.

There appears to be a relationship between the presence of blooms of blue green algae and some red bacteria or algae and the discomfort and even death of fish. Again, whether or not this is related to spores (in the case of red algae) is unknown. With blue green algae there is the possibility that trouble is caused by poisons they release into the water. When sickness and death occur in the presence of blue green algae, it has been noted that neither the protein skimmer nor the subsand filter seem to be effective in preventing the problem. This indicates that the poisonous agent may be dissolved and in a form that cannot be removed by these devices or that during a bloom it builds up too fast to be dealt with.

Typical symptoms of trouble associated with algae and/or bacteria may develop as follows: The first indications of their presence are the appearance of red or blue green spots or smears on the surfaces of glass, shells, corals and other cover. As with most blooms the spots grow slowly for three or four days or longer and then begin to spread rapidly across the surfaces on which they are growing. Up until they begin to expand rapidly there is little change in the behavior of the fish. However, within a day or two after surfaces are largely covered, some fish may become hesitant about feeding. If the bloom is allowed to remain, fish stop feeding and hide instead of swimming around actively. Conversely, some species may become active and swim around appearing to seek a way out of the aquarium. The fish's health begins to deteriorate, colors may fade, fins may become ragged and spots and other signs of disease may appear. Some species may show little visible signs except for the changes in behavior noted. Around this time, they begin to die.

It should be emphasized that an algal or bacterial bloom need not have the consequences noted above. The problem is made difficult because plants may react in different ways at different times. The blue greens, for instance, may or may not be poisonous at times and the conditions governing this are obscure. With this group, coloration can even change from blue green to red under certain conditions of lighting. Depending on the size of the aquarium, the amount of life contained in it, temperature, kinds and efficiency of filtration and other factors, blooms in general may or may not cause problems. However, it is safest for the beginner to treat all blooms as potential trouble and to control growths in the aquarium before they reach such proportions.

It is likely that potential bloom problems can be bypassed safely if one uses an ultraviolet filter (which is different from the UV bulbs used to light aquariums). These units are commercially available and commonly employ a germicidal bulb within a box or tube through which aquarium water flows. The short-wave UV rays from the bulb destroy or alter organic materials in the water, which seems to reduce many of the problems with water quality in marine aquariums. If fish become unhealthy (see "Diseases") around the time that algae are becoming well established, it is advisable to install a UV filter and to let it run continuously. This instrument can be used from the time the aquarium is first set up as one of the permanent components of the system. Although it is a powerful tool in helping to develop and maintain good water quality, it should not be considered a cure-all and used to the exclusion of other components of the system. Many observations have indicated that the protein skimmer, in particular, is an indispensable tool for all but the most experienced marine aquarists.

Another way of reducing problems from blooms is to use activated charcoal. The continual use of this material is recommended beginning at about the time algae and other growth begin to cover coral, tubes and other objects in the aquarium. Use is not recommended when the aquarium first is set up because of possible interference with the establishment of bacteria in the sand. Activated charcoal principally removes dissolved organic materials, some of which are harmful to fish at certain concentrations. This material should be used in the form of small granules which present many absorptive surfaces to which contaminants adhere. Small cylinders filled with activated charcoal that fit over airlift tubes are available and are handy to use. More thorough removal can be achieved by installing an outside filter provided with a thick bed of activated charcoal. The bed should be covered by a one-inch layer of Orlon or glass wool to help reduce overloading the charcoal. The motor that operates the outside filter will pass a large quantity of water which will quickly expose all of the water in the aquarium to the action of the activated charcoal. The filter can be run continuously and also will provide a good current of water within the aquarium, which is desirable. Activated charcoal should be changed about once every three or four weeks as its usefulness declines over time.

It must be kept in mind that the problem with algae and bacteria seems to be associated with blooms which are built up rapidly in many of these plants. If such organisms seem to cover glass, coral and other objects at a more or less steady rate over a period of weeks, a problem is less likely to occur. It also seems that once growth has covered coral and other objects (except for their under-surfaces where light is reduced) and the bloom phase is over, trouble from this source is less likely to appear. If the aquarist has the time and patience to set up his aquarium with invertebrate animals (crabs, anemones, shrimps, etc.) and let the algae and bacteria cover the objects within, problems from this source will probably be greatly reduced. He should keep his animals well fed

Camouflaged head of scorpionfish disguises this predator from its prey. *Courtesy, William M. Stephens*

during this period since the food he introduces will ultimately feed the algae and bacteria so they can multiply. (Note: Algal growth can be slowed by reducing the amount of daylight reaching the aquarium or using a Plant Light or other bulb that is not designed to promote growth.)

Although growth may not spread as quickly after an aquarium is balanced, blooms still can occur if conditions change. An aquarium that has done well all winter can suddenly (or so it seems) break out with an algal bloom in late winter or early spring. This is due to a subtle increase in the length of day that occurs at this time of year. This occurs in an aquarium that has some exposure to natural daylight, and the reader is cautioned to watch for this situation. It is possible that installing different lighting in a room also may lead to a similar situation.

SCAVENGERS AND HEALTHY AQUARIUMS

An important procedure for maintaining healthy aquariums and fish is to include marine animals that will aid in removing uneaten food. Having a cleaning crew at work at all times within the aquarium helps reduce labor for the aquarist and prevent trouble. The value of this procedure has been known for a long time, but has not been applied with much success. The major reason for this is that marine aquariums traditionally are treated with copper to control many fish diseases and with algae-controlling chemicals that are poisonous to invertebrate animals.

The system used here, except in rare instances, does not employ the use of chemicals because it is based on procedures involving ecological regulation that keep fish in a healthy condition; hence, chemicals are not needed. The system, therefore, permits the use of invertebrates as cleaners which further strengthens its power of self-regulation.

The choice of invertebrate animals for this purpose must be made with care. Crabs are excellent scavengers because they have voracious appetites. They also roam all over an aquarium continually sorting out large to very fine particles from the sand and exploring cracks and crevices. However, crabs also are predators and will eat fish when they can catch them. In an aquarium fish have few places to which they can escape, especially at night when some of them become quiet on the bottom. The choice of crabs to put into the aquarium, therefore, must be taken into consideration.

One should avoid using the common swimming crabs found abundantly along coastlines in the summertime. These long-clawed species which burrow in the sand are

Banded coral shrimp—a handsome occupant of a marine aquarium that will keep it clean. *Courtesy, Wometco Miami Seaquarium*

Swimming crab—a type not compatible with most aquariums. *Courtesy, Wometco Miami Seaquarium*

voracious predators highly capable of catching fish in an aquarium. It is tempting to use very young ones up to one inch across the shell since they are small and relatively weak and do not present much of a hazard to fish. However, in an aquarium they eat a great deal of leftover food and grow at a fast rate. They also hide under the sand and there is a tendency to forget them. Their presence usually is remembered after a time when fish begin to disappear and the aquarist realizes the crab has grown much larger and is supplementing its diet with fish. They are almost impossible to find in an aquarium and one usually has to dismantle it and rake the sand to find them. The large-clawed, slow-moving rock crabs are better candidates, but only small ones should be used because larger individuals have a tendency to move objects around and require more food which the aquarist is trying to keep to a minimum.

The hermit crabs, on the other hand, are ideal as scavengers. These animals occur in tropical and temperate areas where they can be found in both shallow, wadable and deep water. They live in snail shells which they carry around on their "backs" and are very active. Besides being good scavengers they are good climbers and when in an aquarium they scour the branches of coral and climb pipes eating any food they encounter. They are attractive animals, interesting to watch, and their claws are small, which will help to put the aquarist somewhat at ease. Hermit crabs seldom catch and eat fish, but when they do it usually occurs when the latter are in a weakened condition. If a fish dies in an aquarium they soon pounce upon it and devour it, which is a help to the aquarist who does not check his aquarium often enough.

Practically any size of hermit crab can be used. One or two large ones and some smaller individuals make a good balance because the former eat more whereas the latter

Hermit crab—an important occupant of a marine aquarium.
Courtesy, Wometco Miami Seaquarium

can enter small spaces to obtain waste food. A half dozen
will keep an aquarium with 4 or 5 square feet of bottom
very clean. It should be remembered that these little animals shed their skeletons including the legs and antennae
like any other crabs as they grow and these "casts" occasionally will be found in the aquarium. Their presence
usually alarms people who do not know about this habit
as they think the crab has died when they see the "cast"
lying on the sand.

Extra shells in the aquarium will provide new homes
for those that have shed if they have outgrown their
shells. Normally, hermit crabs use shells they select on the
basis of weight, size and other features, so it is best to pro-

vide shells that are not unusually heavy. When they are hard pressed to find a larger shelter, however, they will accept new shells that are larger than they normally prefer if none others are available. If they are forced to vacate their shells and do not find others, they may be eaten by fish that attack their defenseless grublike bodies.

Crabs should be introduced to the aquarium in a manner similar to that used for fish, except that the time can be cut in half. They should not be soaked in water containing chemicals which may injure or kill them. At least some microscopic organisms probably can be removed by placing crabs in fresh water for a few minutes immediately before introducing them into the aquarium. Crabs are hardy animals, but there is no reason to expose them to undue stress if it is unnecessary. Whether or not they carry organisms that may infect fish is questionable, but decontamination may remove undesirable algae or other marine life that clings to them. Hermit crabs often have shells that are overgrown to some degree by algae, barnacles or other marine animals. These should be scraped off before they are decontaminated in fresh water.

CLEANING CORAL AND OTHER OBJECTS

Occasionally one should clean growths from the aquarium. The easiest way to clean objects that are overgrown with algae is to immerse them in a solution of Clorox and water. This material is readily available and can be diluted in proportions of about 1 cup to 10 gallons of fresh water. Coral that is covered lightly with growth will bleach within five to ten minutes, but heavy coatings will take longer. This process also removes small particles of food that sometimes are hidden in crevices. Shells with a shiny finish should be wiped clean as the bleach may dull their surfaces. Bleaching should be carried out in the vicinity of a water tap and drain since large amounts are used. It is better to have a large container so all objects can be treated at once with room left over to prevent spills. Plastic 20-gallon waste cans make good containers for bleaching.

After objects are clean, rinsing can be handled in several ways. If the objects are relatively nonporous, they can be rinsed with a hose or under a faucet for a minute or two making sure the water is squirted all over them. If objects such as coral are being rinsed, they should be set aside to drain for five minutes after being removed from the bleach. This usually is done anyway, since it takes some minutes to empty the container of Clorox and refill it with fresh water. After this they can be submerged and left for about the same time in clean fresh water. This procedure is necessary so the bleach that remains within the many porous spaces of the coral will be diluted by the fresh water as it fills them up. After the coral is removed from the rinse water it should be drained again for about five minutes. Be aware that Clorox is very poisonous to marine life, so objects must be thoroughly rinsed. If any odor of chlorine remains after they are rinsed, they should receive the same treatment again, especially if one has a small aquarium that will not adequately dilute any remaining Clorox when the objects are reintroduced.

GENERAL INSTRUCTIONS ON MAINTAINING THE AQUARIUM

While the hood is off, the top of the aquarium should be inspected to see where deposits of salt and drops of water have built up. Salt can be scraped back into the aquarium if it does not look dirty from accumulated dust. If salt deposits have built up in particular locations on the splash plates, especially where they meet the glass, the gap between the two may be too great. A thin ribbon of silicone rubber can be drawn along the edge of the splash plate to fill this gap. Fumes from this material probably are toxic to fish before it dries, so it should be allowed to set for a few hours in moving air to rid it of most of the fumes. The splash plates can be cleaned with fresh water and reinserted after the inspection is made.

An aquarium should be checked daily to detect the earliest signs of change in the filters, water, temperature, fish and the like. A good time to do this is when the fish are fed. The most crucial daily observation is to see that the protein skimmer is operating properly. At a time when the hood is off, the water coming from the spout can be watched and then can be observed through the glass to see how far it plunges beneath the surface. With this comparison, one can later watch the flow of bubbles plunging beneath the surface from outside and will know how fast it is coming from the spout. With practice it is possible to tell whether or not the mass of bubbles in the main column is "full" enough, indicating that the filtration rate is high. If the bubbles are dense against the sides of the column, the rate is good. If there are few extending to the sides, then the hood will have to be taken off and more air released through the air block (see page 5) . Another criterion of good bubble flow is to watch to see if they fill the chambers of the grid that partially extends below the surface of the water. If there is only a thin layer several bubbles in thickness above the surface in the grid, the rate can be increased a little.

Occasionally, clogging of wooden air breakers is encountered in protein skimmers that utilize them. In contrast to larger bubbles that are produced with normal aging (after several months) the volume released by the air breaker decreases noticeably after as little as two weeks. When additional air applied by opening the valve wider fails to increase the rate of bubble production, it is probable that bacteria (and possibly other microorganisms) have multiplied in the small tubes within the air breaker slowing the rate of flow. When this occurs, one may feel colorless slime coating the inside of the skimmer tube and other tubing and surfaces in the vicinity. The glass walls of the aquarium at times may become coated with this slime, although such growths do not always clog wooden air breakers. A further test to see if clogging has occurred is to increase the air flow to the airlift portion of the skimmer. If this flow is strong and closing it off still will not increase the flow in the air breaker, the latter is obviously clogged.

Replacing a clogged air breaker with a new one will cause the skimmer to operate normally but only for a short while since bacteria will build up again. The only way to ultimately solve the problem is to rid the aquarium of the bacteria. Their numbers might be decreased by using agents such as copper or antibiotics, but these methods may also destroy needed bacteria and other organisms. The problem is a complex one and is best tackled by the beginner by dismantling the aquarium and starting over. The water and sand should be removed and the glass walls, filter plates and tubing cleaned with a brush. The skimmer should be cleaned, taken apart and laid in the bottom of the aquarium. The latter then is filled with fresh water into which two cups of Clorox is mixed (in a 30-gallon aquarium). This should sit for two or three days and then everything should be thoroughly rinsed until the smell of Clorox no longer can be detected. The sand also should be immersed in Clorox in a separate container and treated as above. This must be

Goose barnacles extend netlike structures to snag particles from aquarium water. *Courtesy, William M. Stephens*

very thoroughly washed and may have to be air dried for a few days to eliminate the Clorox. It is preferable to discard the sand and use a new supply, if possible. The aquarium can be set up again as previously outlined. However, it is desirable to inoculate it with material from a different source than formerly or the same situation may occur again. The aquarist should not be apprehensive about the above problem as it rarely occurs.

It sometimes is possible to look through food introduction holes in the hood and see the level of waste in the cup on top of the skimmer. If not, the hood can be tilted (unless a door is installed) daily to make sure the cup is not too full. Occasionally, a cup will overflow because too high a rate of air flow has occurred in the bubble chamber. Although this situation is not as bad as having a slow accumulation overflow, it should be avoided.

Occasionally, at feeding time one should squirt water into coral heads, between rocks and into other tight spaces using the syringe arrangement. It is hard for crabs and fish to get food in such places and it often can be dislodged by the strong current of water from the syringe. This practice only takes a minute, but is one of the techniques that helps to maintain good water quality.

SALINITY

It is important to keep the salinity in the aquarium from becoming higher than about 36 parts per thousand. The chief cause of this is evaporation. When this occurs, the water gets saltier as the level falls because the many elements contained in seawater are left in the aquarium. Increased salinity places fish under stress by making their body processes work harder, weakens them and results in their becoming more susceptible to diseases. It also produces a different environment for bacteria and algae which may undergo changes and in turn change the water quality. All of these changes add to each other and reduce the fish's chances for survival in the aquarium. A drop in water level, therefore, must be compensated as soon as possible.

At the time of feeding, the water level can be noted. Although a lower level due to evaporation is seldom detectable on a daily basis, it can change noticeably over a few days. The rate at which water evaporates varies with a number of factors, the most important being the dryness of the air in the room which houses the aquarium. In a humid climate, evaporation is slow and water may not have to be added for two weeks. However, in inland areas where the climate is dry, it may be necessary to add water once each week. In air conditioned rooms the rate of evaporation is also fast since the air is very dry. Having the salinity a little less than that found in natural seawater (see "Filling the Aquarium") gives a built-in safety factor in case the aquarist forgets to add water.

All that is necessary to correct the effects of evaporation is to add fresh water. To be safe, one can add distilled water. Water from a tap is probably safe, although when it is used there is always the question of whether it is the culprit when trouble develops in the aquarium. Since a drop in water level usually is detected soon after it occurs, it is not generally necessary to add much fresh water to make up the deficit. The small amount that is added is a small proportion of the total and so is greatly diluted. It is likely that harmful materials that may be added along with fresh tap water will be chemically or physically removed before other additions must be made, so the likelihood of them building up to dangerous amounts may be small. Merely bring the water level up to the mark that was put on the aquarium glass when it was first set up. Adding new corals and other objects used as cover may change the water level, since they may displace more or less water than those that were present in the beginning. These amounts usually are relatively small and if they are less than at first, more fresh water can be added. Salinity in the aquarium can be checked with a hydrometer, an inexpensive piece of equipment that can be found in most aquarium stores.

Never replenish evaporated water in the aquarium with salt water. This leads to a continual increase in salinity which under certain circumstances can occur quickly in a small aquarium.

TEMPERATURE

Fish living in an aquarium set up according to the techniques described here are able to withstand a wide range of temperatures. Tropical species do well at temperatures from about 75 to 80 degrees F. They can withstand temperatures slightly below this and considerably above it. As a matter of practice it is best to keep fish at the recommended temperatures. However, if fish are exposed to slowly rising seasonal temperatures, they will become acclimated and then can stand summer hot spells. Large temperature changes over short periods of time should be avoided. A rise or fall in temperature of 10 to 15 degrees F within an hour may be damaging. In air conditioned rooms there is less of a problem since the temperature remains more or less level and a thermostat keeps it stable.

Of great importance is how fast temperature in an aquarium changes. This is determined by three main factors: (1) the difference between temperature in the aquarium and outside it; (2) the size of the aquarium; and (3) how fast and how much air is pumped into it. A large difference in temperature increases the speed with which the water temperature changes. Since there is less water in a small aquarium, its temperature changes faster than a larger one. The use of both a protein skimmer and airlifts operating subsand filters greatly accelerates the speed with which the water changes temperature (over that which occurs when diffusion alone is operating).

Keeping these details in mind will help in dealing with changes in temperature. For instance, if the temperature changes drastically, the rate of change in an aquarium can be slowed by turning off the protein skimmer for a while. The airlifts supplying the subsand filters could be slowed, or stopped for several hours, although this is not good practice because the number of essential bacteria in the sand might be reduced.

Heaters designed for aquariums can be introduced when sustained low temperatures are anticipated. Obtain one that has a good thermostat that permits it to shut off when the desired temperature is reached. It is best to get a heater that has a thermostat that can be placed at a different location in the aquarium (but this is expensive). Types with heater and thermostat combined should be especially watched at least daily over several weeks when temperature changes are occurring to make sure they are operating correctly. A heater that is working improperly can quickly overheat an aquarium and kill the fish. Also make sure the heater capacity is large enough to heat the volume of water in the aquarium (the dealer in a good aquarium shop should have this information). If it is anticipated that room temperatures will drop 5 or more degrees below the recommended temperature, a heater with a greater capacity may be required. A thermometer should always be kept in the aquarium and one also kept in the room will give a comparison showing how the former is reacting to changes in the air temperature.

Most heaters for the home aquarist do not have a device that indicates the setting to use to get a particular temperature. Therefore, it is necessary to find out how far to turn the adjustment that regulates the output of the heater to achieve a desired temperature. After the heater is in the aquarium the adjustment can be turned one way, then the other, until a point is reached where a slight turn will cause it to heat. The position of the adjustment is then set approximately at the existing temperature of the aquarium. One can make a note of this setting to regain this temperature if desired. If the temperature drops below this point, the heater will automatically turn on and bring the temperature up. If a higher temperature is desired, one must turn the heater on with the adjustment control and wait to see the final water temperature that results. This is reached when the heater shuts off. The adjustment should be increased a little at a time to avoid overheating the water.

pH

Changes in the acidity of the water (pH) which lead to harmful consequences usually are not a problem in an aquarium set up as outlined here. The high calcium content sand used results in the strong buffering needed to provide the proper environment for tropical marine fishes. If shells and especially corals also are used as cover in the aquarium, they provide additional calcium as they slowly dissolve. Chemical changes and metabolic activities of organisms in an aquarium can cause lowering of pH with subsequent harm to animal life. Although fishes will tolerate a range in pH from about 7.5 to 8.2, changes from the higher to lower levels must occur slowly over a period of weeks. Blooms of algae and bacteria may cause relatively abrupt lowering of pH, and gradual coating of the sand grains by dissolved organic materials may do so more gradually. The various components of and practices for keeping marine aquariums outlined in this book make it unlikely that pH will fall below about 7.8. Inexpensive kits that give reasonably accurate readings of pH can be purchased.

CHANGING WATER

A schedule for changing part of the water in an aquarium should be followed as an additional safeguard against buildup of contaminants, depletion of trace elements, changes that might influence pH, etc. Draining about one-third of the water from the aquarium about once every six weeks and replacing it with newly acquired water is sufficient. If natural seawater is used, follow the procedures outlined in the section on water, page 9, to prevent introducing undesirable microorganisms and other material. Although this may seem like a rather large proportion to change, it can be added all at once with no observable effect on the fish. Aquarium fish held under good conditions easily can withstand changes of this proportion and even larger ones.

Water changes can be carried out conveniently by siphoning the required amount into a container of known capacity such as a 5-gallon plastic can. In this way, it is possible to keep track of how much has been removed so no more is withdrawn than the supply available for refilling. Some of the water withdrawn should be retained until the aquarium is refilled as a portion of this can be readded in case there has been a miscalculation. If the end of the hose is moved around close to the bottom, accumulated detritus can be siphoned off as water is removed. The detritus particles eventually will settle out on the bottom of their container so the water can be reused, if needed. A hose one-half to three-fourths inch inside diameter will speed this operation.

LIGHTING THE AQUARIUM

Properly lighting an aquarium is important because of its relationship with microscopic plant life that in turn is related to water quality (see "Plant Growth in the Aquarium," page 60) . When an aquarium first is set up, it is best to allow lights to burn about eight or ten hours each day if no natural lighting is present. After about a month, lighted periods can extend into the evening as long as desired. Remember that plants will grow in response to both artificial and natural light, so it may be necessary to reduce the former if the aquarium is near a window where the latter is strong. If possible, try to regulate the total amount of light so that algae grows and covers objects at a fairly steady rate rather than "exploding" as a bloom over a few days' time. When the objects in the aquarium are overgrown after two months or more, the effects of increased or decreased amounts of light are not as noticeable and may appear as increases or decreases in the density of the algae that is present. Changes in density sometimes occur when bulbs grow weaker over a period of months and algae may look less green or brown depending on the kind that is present. Replacing an old with a new one likely will deepen the color soon afterward.

As has been stated, the idea behind first lighting an aquarium is to produce a growth of algae gradually. This can be done preferably by using a fluorescent GroLux (Sylvania) or a Plant Light (GE) bulb. The former bulb is designed to promote plant growth and will do so quickly. Therefore, it might be necessary to "shade" the bulb to slow the growth. The latter bulb will enhance colors of fish and other objects in the aquarium as will the GroLux, but it is not designed to promote plant growth. This bulb probably will not have to be shaded. Ordinary daylight bulbs can be used and will promote growth to some extent, but they tend to "wash out" colors in the aquarium.

It is possible to reach a compromise between dim and bright lighting by using a simple technique. Aluminum foil wrapped around one bulb in a two-bulb fixture will prevent light from leaving it. Different amounts of light can be permitted to leave the bulb by wrapping only part of it. It can, for instance, be wrapped in two places so light will shine from the two ends and the middle of the bulb giving some illumination to the ends and middle of the aquarium. Regulating the width of the wrapping will prevent strongly lighted zones in the middle and ends of the aquarium. The edges of the aluminum foil should be taped so they do not unroll from the bulb. Small pieces of Scotch tape are useful for this purpose and serve to insulate the foil from electrical contacts.

The foil should be checked every two weeks or so to make sure it has not deteriorated from the action of the salt-laden air within the hood. When this begins, the foil can be removed and a new piece inserted. A glass tube inserted over the foil-wrapped bulb will reduce deterioration and will prevent any corrosion products that might develop from falling into the water. Other methods of protecting the foil can be devised, but it should be remembered that bulbs get somewhat hot so materials that melt or smolder should not touch them. Strips of adhesive Mylar also can be used since they are nonconductive and noncorrosive.

Other types of bulbs that can be used are long-wave ultraviolet and those that produce red light. The former has been dealt with under "Initial Lighting," page 50. The latter produce a dim red glow that will light the aquarium at night when all other lights have been extinguished. Fish that retire after dark will not swim around when this light is used, but it will not prevent cardinals and other night-roving species from performing their nocturnal activities. A striking effect can be achieved by using red light in an aquarium stocked with nocturnal species of fish. This type of light is not a necessity to view such species, however, as they will become somewhat

Pearlfish slides backward into its home inside a sea cucumber.
Courtesy, William M. Stephens

active during the daytime after they are acclimated to aquarium life. With some species this may take weeks.

CHOOSING FISH

The choice of marine fishes offers a number of thorny problems involving cost, behavior and logistics. All of these factors must be balanced by the aquarist to suit his particular situation. What an aquarist wishes to pay for his fish is up to him, but he should not pay for high-priced fish just because he can afford it. Of more concern is how well fish do in the aquarium, how they affect it and how they behave with others. These questions will be discussed in the next chapter.

6

Behavior
in the Aquarium

There are general rules of behavior the aquarist must learn in order to help him select fish and how many to keep in an aquarium. These include considerations of species, size, aggressiveness and feeding habits. When fish are put into an aquarium and the length of time they remain there have a strong bearing on behavior. Knowledge of these factors is used to "balance" an aquarium for increased activity and attractiveness as well as the more critical aspect of creating the workable harmony that places limits on how many fish can be kept. These considerations will become clear as they are discussed together.

Some species of fish are more aggressive than others. In general, fish are more aggressive toward their own species than toward others and larger individuals are more aggressive than smaller ones. Some damselfish of the same species will attack each other viciously and will kill one another in an aquarium (as will some angelfish and others). They will attack other species of fish, their aggressiveness increasing as they grow larger. Although larger individuals almost invariably are the aggressors, they may be attacked by smaller fish if the latter are established in the aquarium before they are introduced. The larger fish may or may not eventually be able to dominate the smaller ones depending on size and other factors. The closer fish are in size the more viciously they will fight. Fish much smaller in size flee more quickly and thus avoid damaging bites that are the start of trouble from infection and more persistent attacks that eventually may result in death. A fish that is considerably smaller than another usually is not attacked persistently.

Aggressiveness need not result in damage or death. If the smaller fish is able to escape into small spaces between rocks or within other cover where the larger individual cannot reach it, it can survive to live a somewhat harried life occasionally dashing out for food. The tough, territorial damselfish seem to exist reasonably well under these conditions. However, the smaller fish may be driven into an upper corner of the aquarium where it is kept at bay by occasional attacks from its assailant. This attempt to hide may be preceded by rapid swimming up and down the glass and inability to feed. Such a fish occasionally may dash out for food, but essentially is lost to the mainstream of life in the aquarium since it does not participate in activities and usually is not seen at all. In this situation, the fish should be removed, for it may become so cowed it can starve to death rather than eat. Angelfish, butterfly fish, cardinal fish, some damselfish and neon gobies are among those that show this kind of behavior toward their own species and sometimes others.

During feeding, larger individuals may chase others away from food. This problem can be minimized by following instructions in the section on initial feeding. Occasionally, however, one fish will vigorously chase another and the latter may not get enough to eat. In general, though, fish become so interested in food when it is introduced they quickly cease aggressive activities.

With these considerations in mind, one can begin introducing fish into the aquarium (see "Introducing Wild Fish to the Aquarium," page 42). When first introducing fish it is best to keep their numbers and size small until the bacteria become established. A few fish are needed to produce waste products that—together with some of their food—will feed the bacteria so their numbers will increase. Species such as blennies, gobies, wrasses and cardinal fish are good to start with whereas butterfly fish, moorish idols, surgeonfish and similar kinds are less likely to survive at this stage. In an aquarium of about 30-gallon capacity one can first introduce several fish up to about 2 inches in length. Potentially very aggressive species such as the beau gregory should be avoided unless they are an inch or less in size.

After an aquarium has contained fish for a week or more, or when the nitrite level has dropped, it is safe to introduce more fish. At this time, the aquarist can introduce two or three more fish chosen in the light of the foregoing discussion. Aggression by fish already in the aquarium can be forestalled for a short time by introducing food along with the new fish, which diverts attention from them by the old residents. If the aquarist knows little about how different species react toward each other, he can introduce more cover and rearrange that already in the aquarium immediately before he introduces new fish. This helps to disorient old residents and gain time for the new arrivals to adjust. Introducing larger fish each time gives the newcomers an advantage as they will not be attacked as persistently as smaller ones unless a particularly aggressive species is already there.

From the first time fish are introduced, the aquarist must watch them closely. Initially, fish will hide, swim against the glass or lie quietly next to objects in the aquarium. They may continue to behave this way for a matter of hours or for a day. If they have been bought in a store and are partially acclimated to aquarium life, they may begin slowly to explore their surroundings within an hour or two. Wild fish will remain timid for longer periods of time.

An occasional glance at the aquarium will provide spot checks to determine what various fish are doing at times when they are not being fed. If the recommended procedures are followed, little initial aggression will be noticed as the primary "urge" is to explore new quarters. Some low-level aggression probably will occur within a day or two and then tend to decrease.

The aquarist will notice increased swimming and exploratory behavior for a while, but after a few days fish will begin to establish patterns of behavior if they have had previous aquarium experience. They will mostly frequent particular areas within the aquarium, but occasionally will swim to other locations. Some species such as high hats and neon gobies may stay close together, but most will keep different distances between each other. As they become adjusted, they occasionally will briefly dart at each other, but sustained chasing becomes rare. If one has chosen two members of the same species, chasing may persist unless sufficient cover has been provided.

When additional fish are introduced, there will be at least a temporary change in behavior. New fish will be approached and possibly chased as noted above. However, if attacks do not persist, the newcomers become fairly well adjusted within a day or two. Again, the aquarist should closely observe this period of adjustment to learn the behavior of the fish and detect undue aggression.

By starting with the proper species and sizes of fish, the aquarist is beginning to develop a behavioral balance enabling him to determine the number of fish a given aquarium ultimately can hold. There is little problem achieving this when only a few fish are present because space limitations are not great and fish can stay away from one another enough to reduce aggression. However, as numbers and species increase they are forced to associate more closely with one another and aggression increases. With increasing numbers of fish the aquarist must pay more attention and employ additional techniques to maintain harmony.

After four or five fish are in the aquarium, wait until their behavior has stabilized before adding more fish. This is apparent when they remain in the same locations or swim around in a manner which seems to be typical

Scrappy beau gregory pauses among feathery algae in its aquarium home. *Courtesy, William M. Stephens*

for them. The same fish chase the ones they always chase with about the same low level of aggression. When they are fed, most of them rush to get the food and the same ones that always wait until the food comes to them still behave this way. Subsequent to being fed, fish return to their same activities after a period of searching for remaining food.

Occasionally, a fish appears to want to feed, but does not. If this reticent fish does get a morsel or two and its behavior does not change, it may survive for months. However, if it becomes noticeably thinner and more reluctant to feed, it will eventually weaken and die. One should be cautious of his feeding technique because there is a tendency to overfeed to permit such a fish to get some of the excess food.

It first is necessary to know what a normal fish of a species looks like so a "thin" one can be recognized. When a fish is first caught or purchased it usually is in a more or less well-fed condition. At this time and when fish are first introduced into the aquarium they should be observed closely so the aquarist can become familiar with how "round" they appear. This is most readily observed from a front view when a fish is swimming directly toward the observer's eyes. From this view some species look cigar-shaped whereas others present a double convex shape. When underfed for several weeks fish become thinner through the sides and in some species the top of the head and body may sweep outward like the sides of a tent.

The reason for refusing to eat must be determined if the fish is to survive and become part of the balance of the aquarium. Its behavior must be watched to see if it is being constantly harassed. If a close watch is not kept, one fish can subdue another forcing it to become reclusive and remain that way with little further effort by the aggressor. If the aquarist has missed the foregoing events, all he may see is a fish cowering in a corner for no apparent reason. Actually, with experience one will learn to recognize the occasional "intention" movements of the aggressor in the direction of the subdued fish reminding it that it cannot move for fear of a full-scale attack.

If a fish is overharassed, it may be restored to normal by removing the aggressor for several days to a week and then reintroducing it into the aquarium. Another procedure is to introduce a fish of the same species, but smaller than the aggressive one. In this case, if sufficient cover is available, the aggression may be directed toward the newcomer that is able to exist without too much difficulty since it can escape. This technique sometimes results in both fish being mutually occupied by each other to the extent that others are not attacked as much as if either were alone. On the other hand, this technique could lead to renewed attacks on the subdued fish. A harassed fish can always be removed to another aquarium if one is available.

In other cases where a fish will not feed, it may be noticed that it nonetheless swims freely around and may sample food and reject it or merely look at it without feeding. Again, such a fish represents an imbalance because it eventually will die and the aquarist allows it a certain amount of food that goes uneaten. This problem must be dealt with in a different way from the timid fish that will not eat.

It is assumed that feeding has been carried out according to previous instructions and that the noneater has sampled the "usual" food. If the fish seems in harmony with the others and has never fed, it probably requires a special food or that existing food be presented in a special way. In general. butterfly fish, moorish idols, very small high hats and others have this problem and it is not always possible to "wean" them away from their natural food. However, there are approaches to this problem that help induce fishes to feed.

It is convenient to have a small aquarium set up in which fish can be fed special foods. If this is done in an aquarium containing other fish, a problem of uneaten food or the introduction of new organisms may result. If the nonfeeder will not eat tubifex worms, live brine shrimp, pieces of crab or other foods not normally used, an overgrown rock or piece of living coral from uncontaminated offshore waters can be introduced since most species show an interest in "picking" on such objects. One of the causes of feeding problems in some species is their need to actually pick food from the bottom. Advantage can be taken of their natural inclination to do this by fastening chunks of food to rocks so they have to pull off pieces. Doing this encourages a fish to pick nearby pieces of food from the bottom or the water as this often is done naturally when a fish feeds. These techniques eventually may enable a fish to break the behavioral barriers that bind it to attached food and it then can feed with others. There are other factors involved such as appearance of food, size and motion, but once a fish begins to feed, these often become less important to it.

Another technique used to achieve a balanced aquarium can be provided by taking advantage of natural tendencies of fish to spend their time in particular locations. Fish can be arbitrarily divided into two main groups depending on whether they spend most of their time above the bottom or among rocks and other cover. By utilizing these tendencies, the aquarist can keep more fish in his aquarium than would be possible if this behavior did not exist. Fish that normally live above the bottom will also behave this way in an aquarium and, therefore, are not forced together with those that live on the bottom. Since they do not compete for the same space, aggression is minimized. Being relatively content with an area in which to live is important for aquarium fish and the survival of some is affected by this factor.

This technique for increasing the holding capacity of an aquarium does not prevent aggression, nor does it permit fish to be completely at ease. It results in a low level of aggression that is an advantage rather than a disadvantage because it requires fish to remain active. One of the failings of a marine aquarium is that currents and turbulence found in the natural environment are essentially absent. In captivity, therefore, fish do not get the physical exercise necessary to keep them in good condition and any method that can aid this situation is a valuable supplement to keeping healthy fish.

Regulating the amount of cover can also reduce the level of aggression. Placing most coral, shells or other objects together at one end will sometimes provide a more favorable habitat for an aggressive fish that will spend most of its time there. Other fish will accumulate at the other end where aggression may now be reduced. Increasing the number of objects and piling them over a greater area of the bottom seems to keep some aggressive fish busy swimming among them, which also reduces aggression. Fish that live above the bottom attack each other and also are attacked by those below. Since they cannot retreat to the bottom where they are attacked more vigorously, it is difficult for them to hide from view, thus reducing the level of aggression in the attacking fish. Large, branching corals or comparable objects give some protection for these fish, both helping to prevent attacks and making them shorter in duration.

Because of the behavioral problems that can result, it is unlikely that an aquarist will overload his filtration system. Overharassed fish, torn fins and possibly local infections in wounds resulting from fighting are likely to occur as warning signs of overloading. However, some species of fish that school such as snappers, grunts and some damselfish generally are compatible and might possibly overload as powerful a system as outlined here. An accumulation of too many waste products from the fishes' own body functions often becomes apparent in a constant increase in the amount of material accumulated in the cup on the protein skimmer providing there are no dead fish or other such problems (bear in mind that a skimmer will accumulate a great deal of material after the aquarium has been cleaned).

AQUARIUM CAPACITY AND NUMBERS OF FISH

The question of how many fish an aquarium can hold has no single answer. It depends on (1) the kind, size and numbers of fish; (2) the size of the aquarium; (3) the efficiency of the filtration system ; and (4) the efficiency of the feeding procedures. All of these factors have been discussed along with some of the ways in which they influence each other. The system presented here has been used to construct and maintain 30-, 45-, 80-, and 100-gallon aquariums. Table 1 shows average numbers and sizes of fishes held in these aquariums for at least one year.

TABLE 1

RELATIONSHIP OF AQUARIUM SIZE

AND SIZE AND NUMBER OF FISH

Aquarium size (gallons)	Average fish size (inches)	Numbers of fish
30	2	6
45	2	9
80	2	20
100	2	28

On the average, one-quarter of the fishes held in aquariums were deep-bodied types such as the three-spot damselfish and angelfish and the remainder were more torpedo-shaped types such as the blue demoiselle, grammas and gobies.

From these figures it is easy to calculate how many inches of fish were held in an aquarium. In a 30-gallon aquarium, for instance, there were 2-by-6 or 12 inches of fish. From this it could be calculated that a 30-gallon aquarium could hold two 6-inch fish which would equal 12 inches of fish. However, such figuring is misleading because the volumes (and hence the weight) of many fish increase as a cube of their length. For example, a fish weighing 3 ounces that doubles its length from 2 to 4 inches actually may triple its weight from 3 to 9 ounces. The proportionally greater increase in weight is the critical thing for the aquarist because more fish flesh means it takes more food to feed it and more waste products will be produced. Both of these factors are related to fouling in the aquarium and hence to water quality. When making such calculations, therefore, it is best for the average aquarist to confine his manipulations to fish that are less than about 2½ inches in length. Remember that fish look about one-third larger when underwater so a 3-inch fish appears to be about 4 inches in length.

The author has no doubt that the figures listed in Table 1 are below the carrying capacity of the aquariums. It is likely that half again as many fish as listed can be successfully kept. The aquarist's task is to increase gradually the number of fish in his aquarium to about that in the table. Then he can continue to add one or two fish at a time until constant problems tell him he has exceeded the capacity of his aquarium. Most people will be satisfied with the numbers of fish in their aquariums before this point is reached.

ECOLOGICAL BALANCE

We now have an idea what it means to balance or adjust an aquarium in relation to the behavior of the fish. There also exists an ecological balance of which behavioral balance is only a part. This type of balance is of greater concern and involves good water quality and its maintenance over long periods of time.

Good water quality is not just basic water with nothing in it except the hydrogen and oxygen of which its molecules are composed. For marine fish it is basic water to which has been added a great number of elements such as chlorine, sodium, potassium and calcium to mention only a very few. Also included in seawater are a great number of other chemicals that result from the activities of living organisms. The presence of some of these such as ammonia, nitrites and nitrates are known, and some of their effects on organisms have been determined, or at least suspected. However, the composition of other substances in seawater that promote or inhibit growth are not known and their presence and effects are mostly only suspected. The chemistry of seawater is far more complicated than this and involves how its elements work together to affect living organisms and how such factors as temperature, light, oxygen and others affect the complex.

What we call good water quality in an aquarium is some sort of state that exists between these factors that permit fish to remain in a healthy condition. When this occurs and continues for months at a time, we say that the aquarium is balanced. This does not mean that the water quality never varies. The presence of an algal bloom or cleaning the aquarium changes the chemistry of the water and can have a profound effect on fish. However, healthy fish can tolerate poor water quality until the aquarium

Hermit crab creates part of its own ecology by placing anemones on its shell home. *Courtesy, William M. Stephens*

again reaches the state where materials that are being formed, broken down and reformed produce healthy living conditions. The methods presented in this book are successful because they permit a balance that keeps water quality within limits in which fish can remain healthy.

7

Diseases

Diseases of marine fishes have been the subject of a number of books and articles. This is a specialized subject and will not be discussed here in detail. The aquarist is referred to these other works, some of which are included in the "List of Readings" if he suspects he has a disease problem. However, a few general remarks will be made about disease as it applies to marine aquariums set up by the methods outlined here.

The most usual problem that has been noted is occasional "chafing." Fish approach an object in the aquarium or the bottom and then make a quick dash against it rubbing the area of the gill as they go. It is questionable whether disease organisms always are involved in cases of chafing. This activity has been noted at times when salinity rises above 38 or 39 parts per thousand. It also has been noted at the time that heavy algal blooms occur. Whether conditions in the water irritate the gills or favor an increase in numbers of organisms that infest them is uncertain. Possibly, both occur. Diluting the water to proper salinities often will stop the problem within a few hours. If this fails, or salinities were normal, and if a heavy growth of algae or bacteria had not recently occurred, then disease-producing organisms may be suspect. In this case, a copper sulfate-acetic acid solution added to the aquarium may quickly remove the problem. This can be prepared and added in the following proportions:

Mix two grams of copper sulfate (formula $CuSO_4 \cdot 5H_2O$) with 1 gram acetic acid in 1 quart of water. Mix the ingredients initially in about 1 cup of water to aid in dissolving them. Add 2 millilitres (buy a small graduated cylinder for measuring) per gallon of aquarium water. If the condition is not corrected within about thirty-six hours, double the dose, but add no more than this.

It is safest to remove the crabs and other invertebrates before applying the copper sulfate solution. After the solution has been added to the aquarium at several locations stir the water gently for several minutes. Then turn off the air to the lifts and skimmer for about an hour so the chemicals are not removed too quickly by the subsand filters and possibly the skimmer. Let the air run again for several hours after this before introducing the invertebrates to reduce the concentration of the chemicals. These are mild doses and probably will kill the organisms that might be causing the irritation.

If fish break out in white spots they may have the disease commonly called "ick." This also can be treated with the copper sulfate formula above. The disease is highly susceptible to this treatment and usually is not much of a problem. When ick or gill irritations occur, the aquarist should check to see whether he is using a light bulb that promotes plant growth. Illumination from this type of light seems to aggravate the condition if not actually helping to cause it. This type of light should be discontinued during treatment and reinstated later if the aquarist wishes to see if it has any effect. The best policy, however, is to use a bulb that enhances fish colors without promoting plant growth.

Occasionally, signs of local infections that are confined only to one fish will develop. Fuzzy spots may occur on the body, head, or the edges of fins, and lesions that do not seem to heal may appear. This indicates that the fish is sick, although the aquarium remains healthy as shown by other fish that are normal. In this case, the fish should be removed and treated rather than introducing chemicals into the aquarium.

Catching a fish in an aquarium is almost as difficult as catching one in its natural environment on a reef because a net cannot be worked through the coral and other cover. Fish that are close to death can be caught because they do not not move well and frequently come to the surface. However, one should try to get a fish out before this point is reached in case it has an infectious disease. Removing a fish can be done by the following method, which eliminates the laborious task of removing all of the coral and other cover.

If it has been noted that the (sick) fish hides in a particular shell or other object, try to chase it there and then lift the object out of the water along with the fish. A net held under the object as it comes up through the water and after it is out may prevent the fish from escaping if it leaves its shelter. This method works with some species, but others tend to desert cover as it is lifted from the bottom after they have been in an aquarium for a while. However, this is the best method to try first as it is the easiest.

In the event that this does not work, the aquarium can be drained leaving only a few inches of water in the bottom. The water can be siphoned into a 20- or 30-gallon plastic container with little trouble or loss of water. A net then can be placed in the aquarium and the fish chased into it by hand. This method works because fish no longer can escape the net by swimming over it and the aquarist does not have to move it around causing it to snag on some of the cover. Occasionally it may be necessary to move one or two pieces of cover, which is only a minor inconvenience.

The only real inconvenience to this method of removing fish is putting the water back into the aquarium. It is well worthwhile to purchase a small submersible pump for approximately $20.00 that can be used to return water to the aquarium. Otherwise, it will have to be returned by bucket, which usually leads to some splashing and a greater mess to clean up. When removing water or cover or at times when water is likely to be spilled or splashed, it is a help to lay newspapers in the area of the aquarium.

Treating a fish with potassium permanganate as described in the section on decontaminating will kill many surface infections. If a spot appears on a fish and persists or grows, it can be treated locally. Dip a Q-Tip or similar object in a strong solution of potassium permanganate (dissolve a small piece of tablet or some crystals in a drop of water) and gently scrub the infected area. Make sure to pick up the fish with a wet hand as dry fingers will pull off the protective mucus that covers it, leaving it open to additional infections. This technique of treating an infection can be done quickly if the aquarist has all the materials placed and ready before he picks up the fish. Perform this task over a bucket of water or the aquarium in case the fish slips from the hand.

If a single fish becomes diseased, it probably signifies that for some reason that particular individual is not generally healthy enough to be resistant. However, even when only one fish is involved, the aquarist should scan his list of activities to see what he has done to the aquarium and the fish so he possibly can find an explanation for the trouble. He might, for instance, recently have removed his coral and the fish might have struck and injured itself while it was dashing around. Sometimes the occurrence of an individual diseased or erratic fish is the first warning of general trouble, so such an event should be viewed with concern.

The few remedies described here should take care of most all of the problems encountered. However, if they do not cure a fish, or trouble with different symptoms occurs and the aquarist cannot find his own explanation based on the past history of his aquarium he should consult a book or an experienced aquarist. Something to keep in mind is that fish, like any other living organisms, grow old and may have life spans of only a few years at best. Therefore, it is likely that one occasionally will be confronted with a fish that is deteriorating because of its age or perhaps some weakness in its bodily functions.

RECOGNIZING TROUBLE

The requisites for successfully keeping a marine aquarium have been described. Once the system is operating and routine maintenance has been started the aquarist must remain alert to changes that occur so he can detect the early hint of trouble. There are "signs" within the aquarium that he can "read" which will help him achieve this goal and keep his system healthy.

He begins to lay the foundation for his ability to recognize trouble from the day he sets up his aquarium. After the initial turbidity (if any) has passed, the aquarium water will be at the level at which it will be held and will be crystal clear with no sign of color or even tiny particles. The airlifts that operate the subsand filters will be bubbling at a moderate rate and the protein skimmer at its set rate of delivery. The coral and other objects forming the cover for fish will be perfectly clean and the sand will be undisturbed as yet by the rummaging of the hermit crabs. Fanning the bottom will raise no particles that do not immediately fall back and remain there. The fish will be reacting toward each other in ways that become familiar and will come to food quickly when it is dropped into the water after a few days. The aquarist also will take note of their color and any marks that look as though they are not supposed to be there. The edges of the fins, in particular, should be observed to see that they are sharp, clear, and symmetrical. If the aquarist is not familiar with fish and sees a mark that he may question as being normal, he should look to see if a comparable mark exists in a comparable place on the other side of the fish. Although some infections or marks may appear on both sides of a fish they often occur on only one side, which indicates they are not normal. Observing all these conditions of aquarium and fish and many more of which he will become aware during the construction and maintenance of his system will give the aquarist his base point for comparing the changes that will occur. The rudiments of his ecological system have been established and visible changes will begin to occur.

Among the important events that affect water quality, and therefore fish, are increasing numbers of algal, bacterial and protozoan populations. Algal blooms are usually easy to see and can be followed as they become more dense on the coral and other objects, but bacteria and protozoa may be less easily detected. Bacterial growths on the glass and pipes can be detected because they feel slimy to the touch and huge numbers in the water may make it cloudy. Some large protozoa may be seen with the naked eye, but a buildup in their numbers is less likely to be detected until they affect the fish.

When algal or bacterial populations are small their effect upon the water is little because they remove correspondingly less materials, use less oxygen and add smaller quantities of their own waste products. Their reduced influence continues for days or weeks and then suddenly may increase to bloom proportions. When this occurs they begin to utilize far greater quantities of waste products, but now produce far more of their own. Algae contribute oxygen which is desirable, but not necessary, but they also may release materials that adversely affect fish (see "Plant Growth in the Aquarium," page 60). Because of these conditions the aquarist should closely watch the behavior of the fish if he sees large increases in growths in his aquarium. Sometimes the first sign of such increases may be detectable only as a change in the behavior of the fish. The best policy is to keep algae and bacteria growing slowly until they cover the surfaces of objects in the aquarium.

The procedures of the aquarist are also likely to affect water quality. Forgetting to add water to compensate for evaporation, failing to adjust the flow of water through the protein skimmer, substituting different kinds of lights are among many common causes of ecological shifts that affect water quality. This does not always happen, because the system may be able to absorb some changes without destroying its balance to an appreciable extent. However, if potentially adverse changes are not corrected or a number of them occur together, it is likely that a change in the behavior of the fish will occur.

Although fish perform many different behavioral activities, a few days of close observation will make them familiar enough so that marked changes can be recognized. One of the important signs that fish show in response to ill health is a tendency to cease active swimming and remain in one location. In the early stages, a fish may swim slowly to food without much enthusiasm and eat sparingly, if at all. This behavior deteriorates to a point where it no longer even swims to food, apparently remaining disinterested. It spends most of its time slowly "finning" in one location which often is behind some object. Fish tend to choose darker locations in the aquarium and may remain completely hidden. They may also become timid and withdraw behind shelter at the approach of the aquarist. Occasionally, another fish may chase an ill one from its cover, but the individual will return to seclusion as soon as possible, again becoming quiet. If the situation persists, the fish may become thinner (also noticeable to the aquarist) over a period of weeks and eventually may begin to wander aimlessly around the aquarium. During these periods it often comes into contact with columns of rising bubbles and is swept to the surface where it may remain. A day or two after this behavior, it usually appears to have difficulty maintaining its balance and death may occur soon after. In a weakened condition it may be attacked by other fish which it fails to avoid and eventually it will be caught and eaten by the hermit crabs unless it remains on the surface.

Colors of some species, e.g., rock beauties, royal grammas and some angelfish, fade after they are in an aquarium for one or two months. On the other hand, if fish become sick, fading may occur within a matter of days or even overnight. Bear in mind that changes in color due to aggression, feeding or reproductive activity usually disappear within minutes with the fish resuming its normal coloration after the associated behavior disappears. Color changes may not occur in all species and it is possible that this may or may not occur depending on the nature of

Parasite-picking shrimp lives among the tentacles of a sea anemone. *Courtesy, William M. Stephens*

the ailment. Rock beauties sometimes will die in a healthy aquarium with little fading other than that which appears normal. Royal grammas, on the other hand, have been seen to retain normal coloration and to linger for months after being poisoned in a fouled aquarium. Color should be watched, nonetheless, with these considerations in mind as an indicator of trouble in an aquarium.

Yet another indication of ill health is the tendency for some species to keep the dorsal fin raised. This may occur normally during periods of aggression as a display toward other fish, but like color changes it reverts to a normal (depressed) attitude after the mood has passed. A

continually raised dorsal fin in a sick fish may be associated with a color change as well as a tendency to remain
inactive.

Some species have a tendency to jump out of aquariums apparently as a response to bad water quality that
agitates them. This behavior also may occur when a fish
is attacked persistently by another, but the aquarist may
be aware of such conflict situations which can account for
the behavior. Jawfish, blennies, and blue reef fish are
known jumpers whereas most others jump less frequently.

At times, a group of fish rather than single individuals
show signs of stress. This is a more sure sign that something is wrong with the water quality. Increased swimming, aggression and hiding by a number of individuals
indicate problems. An increase in the speed of swimming,
general activity and aggression, however, are normal
around feeding time, but this decreases after food is
eaten.

Some changes in behavior are of short duration and are
not due to serious problems with water quality. The
aquarist should be acutely aware of happenings within
his aquarium and should make it standard practice to be
particularly watchful for a day or two after he has made
any adjustment to the system. Changes in behavior are
rapid when new fish are introduced. The older residents
characteristically rush over to newcomers and attack or
inspect them. The latter show little inclination to defend
themselves and wander around bewildered in their new
surroundings or hide. Unless a particularly aggressive
individual is involved, both old and new residents usually
are swimming around by the next day with more or less
stabilized behavior patterns.

Fish acclimated to aquarium life usually return almost immediately to their normal routines after the
aquarium has been cleaned. If new objects have been

introduced, some species will briefly explore them whereas others that are more territorial may prolong this activity and adjust their territories to some extent. A group of fish that have been living together for a period of several weeks become very familiar with each other and even aggressive species tend to become more tolerant. Fish that have lived together and are moved to another aquarium tend to maintain this relationship, which probably helps them adjust to the new situation.

Changing the conditions in an aquarium can lead to problems that are reflected in changes in the behavior of fish; these may appear some days or weeks after an adjustment has been made. A number of steps can be followed that will help to determine the cause of trouble shown by unusual behavior. After making sure fish are not temporarily reacting to one another, they should be observed for signs of disease. If lesions, growths, etc., are present, then part of the problem becomes apparent. It is probable that changes in water quality have led to the problem so the aquarist must look further. Make sure all of the components of the aquarium such as filters, lights and especially the protein skimmer are working properly. Try to recall whether they were in order within the last day or two. Reestablishing the proper operation of components such as these often leads to normal behavior within a day or two indicating the trouble has been corrected and the water quality has improved. The water level and temperature should be checked and restored if they are not normal. Here again, correcting such conditions may result in quickly bringing the fish back to normal. The salinity may be checked although it is unlikely to vary much. The pH also can be checked, but it also is unlikely that this will be a problem. If there has been a rapid increase in amount of algae in the aquarium over the previous few days, abnormal behavior may be the result of imbalances related to this and the plant population should be reduced or an ultraviolet filter added. Finally, if these steps do not improve the condition of the fish the aquarist should consult a log (which he should keep to show when he made what changes) to see what other changes he has made in the aquarium that might influence it. When fish are behaving with a high degree of abnormality, a condition that can develop overnight, it is advisable to immediately drain about one-half to one-third of the water and replace it. Even though the source of the trouble may be recognized and corrected, it may take the water a day or more to recover and if fish are in poor condition they may not live until this happens unless some of the water is changed.

When fish are visibly diseased or behave in a way that indicates organisms are involved, they must be treated (see "Diseases") if the above procedures fail to reduce the symptoms in a few days. Whether or not fish show visible signs of disease, changes in water quality should be suspected as causing abnormal behavior. If the airlifts that operate the subsand filters seem to be operating properly and there are visible signs that algae are growing on the glass and other objects, then one can reasonably assume that the sand has a population of organisms and is doing its job both as a physical and biological filter. A strong positive test for nitrite means an imbalance among essential bacteria and is a likely explanation for problems with fish. This particular test has been singled out because kits are available that show levels of this form of nitrogen. Tests for ammonia would be better, but are complex, costly and not available to the average person.

Filtration by the protein skimmer leaves visible indications of conditions by the amount of material that it collects. If the amount of material collected within a few days or a week suddenly increases, then an excess of some dissolved or suspended material is being produced in the aquarium by fishes, crabs, excess food, microorganisms, or a combination of these or possibly by other factors. The skimmer usually produces large bubbles in the collecting chamber as it removes material shortly after fish are fed, but this is a normal situation that slows and ceases within hours. Activities that disturb the sand load the water with undesirable materials and cause the skimmer to become active. The skimmer will remove these materials. A drop in its output means water quality has improved.

Most of the time the aquarist will find one or more things he has or has not done and that, when rectified, will restore normal conditions. Fish may respond quickly to corrective changes as stated or they may show improvement only after several days. If one has exhausted the list of possible sources of trouble, including a thorough cleaning, and if the aquarium has all the signs of being healthy, then his fish may have been permanently disabled by previously abnormal conditions. If water quality remains bad for a period of time, some fish appear to become blind or unresponsive to conditions around them. This appears to be triggered by sudden changes such as temperature variations that affect fish already weakened (but showing no visible signs) by unhealthy water. Blind fish bump into objects, swim slowly, and although they appear to sense food in some way, cannot find it. Other fish appear to be able to see, but remain unresponsive unless prodded by the aquarist or other fish. It is possible that bad water quality, harmful lighting (some people suspect that short-wave ultraviolet lights may cause fish to become blind) or a sudden improvement in conditions after a long period of bad water quality create such problems. Somewhere within the ecology of the aquarium, physiological problems sometimes are created that can disable fish permanently or for long periods of time. Continued good health of new fish introduced to an aquarium is proof that the trouble that disabled prior residents has been rectified.

EFFECT OF OBJECTS IN THE AQUARIUM

Coral and other objects can be put into aquariums and arranged in various ways that are pleasing to the eye and can be made to correspond to arrangements found in various books. The furnishings that are put into an aquarium depend on the preferences of the aquarist, but there is a more serious aspect to objects placed in aquariums because they become part of the environment and must be considered as they affect the system.

Objects have an effect on the behavior and therefore the well-being of fish. When they are first introduced to aquarium life, fish are very frightened and the presence of good shelter is important to them. However, after they become acclimated they are less dependent on shelter and adjustments of objects can be made. "Introducing Wild Fish to the Aquarium," page 42, can be consulted for details of these relationships.

It is necessary to consider the effects on sanitation of objects placed in the aquarium. Although many procedures have been designed to assure that there will be a minimum of contamination in the aquarium from uneaten food, it is important to use every means possible to achieve this goal. Therefore, when considering objects to be introduced as cover for fish or for decoration, one should keep to a minimum corals and other objects which have many closely spaced branches in which food can accumulate. Objects piled on top of each other also create similar trouble spots. Even though the aquarist can help

The cowfish makes an interesting aquarium inhabitant, but may produce a poisonous slime when under stress. *Courtesy, William M. Stephens*

this situation through cleaning, it adds to the work. If he wishes to have such objects, he should squirt water into them with a syringe or place them where food is less likely to settle into them.

Another potential source of trouble is created by introducing flat objects that effectively remove part of the area that can be serviced by the subsand filter. The greater the surface area of the sand covered by objects, the less effective is the subsand filter. Large individual flat rocks are especially bad, as an excess of hydrogen sulfide-producing bacteria may build up in the sand under them in the stagnant conditions that result from the reduced flow of water. If such objects are used, they should be propped in a way that permits water to be drawn under most of their area by the filter.

The use of plastic decorations is widespread among freshwater aquarists and is gaining popularity among their marine counterparts. Precautionary measures should be taken when using such decorations because they may introduce toxic chemicals into the water. Before they are immersed they should be checked to see if there is any exposed metal. Patches (usually on stems) where metal is not covered by plastic can be sealed with silicone rubber and after this has dried for an hour or two the whole decoration should be immersed for a few days in salt water that is agitated by a stream of air or by other means. Stirring helps to facilitate the loss of chemicals from surfaces before the decoration is introduced into the aquarium. The safest procedure is to withdraw metal wire stem supports completely and weight the bottom of the plant with inert material or affix to existing stone or coral.

Remember that bushy decorations are traps for food particles that may be inaccessible to crabs. The behavior of fish should be watched carefully for a few weeks after plastic decorations are introduced in case toxic substances are building up in the water. If fish appear abnormal, remove the decoration and replace one-half to two-thirds of the water. Always keep in mind, however, that if a problem develops it may not be related to the decoration, so look for other causes as well. This can be said of any problem that develops. It is reasonable to start looking for the source with a relatively recent event, but the cause may lie elsewhere.

A very important point to keep in mind is that artificial plants as well as corals offer many surfaces where bacteria and algae can build up. This means that any bloom that occurs will be much larger than if only solid objects are included in the aquarium. A larger bloom more quickly loads the water with waste products or other materials that may affect fish in unknown ways. Production of microscopic reproductive bodies that may affect the gills of fishes occur suddenly in vast numbers under bloom conditions. Buildup of algae, therefore, should be watched especially carefully in an aquarium containing objects with many surfaces. This along with the other problems connected with plastic decorations makes their use questionable.

8

Other Marine Life

The aquarist can successfully keep many other kinds of marine life in his aquarium. Good water quality and the lack of chemicals in the water provide an environment in which large algae, mollusks, shrimps, worms and other organisms will survive for long periods of time. All of these organisms, however, should be introduced only as they fit in with the balance that first has been established with fish, unless one is interested only in an aquarium containing algae and/or invertebrates. Limitations with certain organisms do exist and must be taken into consideration lest they change the environment in the aquarium. Keep in mind, also, that any organism put into an aquarium should be healthy.

Different kinds of bushlike algae have different requirements for light as do the kinds discussed that create blooms and encrust the inside of the aquarium. If the aquarist uses growth-promoting lights or has his aquarium near a window where bright daylight or sunlight enters, his green algae will do well. Red or brown algal plants will do well in somewhat dimmer light as well as in brighter light. Before placing algae in an aquarium they should be swirled vigorously in fresh water to rid them of particles. If they turn pale or white after remaining in the aquarium for some days, they should be

The arrow crab is an awe-inspiring and easily kept inhabitant for aquariums. *Courtesy, William M. Stephens*

removed as they are dying or dead. Only small quantities should be introduced so all the parts can be watched to determine whether or not it is going to survive. A large amount of algae that quickly dies may rapidly increase the pollution load in the aquarium. Since some red algae and blue greens are poisonous, it probably is better not to introduce these types into an aquarium.

Anemones often are included in aquariums where they do well. When they are introduced they should be acclimated the same way as fish, but should not be exposed to chemical decontamination since this might kill or injure them. They may have to be fed, and thus create a pollution problem if too much food is used. They will eat most of the food that fish eat and will clean up leftover food if it falls upon their surfaces. Normally, food can be dropped gently onto their tentacles or deposited there using the syringe and glass tube. This offers a controlled way of introducing food so it doesn't float elsewhere. Anemones should be pried loose from rocks very carefully without injury to their bases when they are collected and should be placed on hard surfaces in the aquarium. If they do not expand and feed within a week or two they should be removed as they probably are not going to survive. Anemones must be provided with daily illumination or they will not do well.

Problems often are encountered in keeping shrimp. Small shrimps of almost any kind stand little chance when included with even the smaller reef fishes; larger predatory species will attack and eat them immediately. This is unfortunate because shrimps are good scavengers and can help to keep an aquarium clean if they are not molested. Large shrimps of the type normally eaten by people are somewhat immune to attack because of their size and also because they bury in sand for hours at a time. Some species remain buried during the daytime and emerge at night to feed, which further reduces their chances of being eaten by fish.

Although banded coral shrimps usually are not eaten in their natural environment where they clean parasites from fishes, those in aquariums may be attacked. If they are provided with holes large enough to accommodate their legs and antennae as well as their bodies, they will fare better. They are particularly vulnerable when they molt their hard outer shell and must at this time have good protective cover. As with anemones, they should be acclimated slowly without being exposed to chemical decontaminants.

Marine worms, many of which are colorful and interesting to watch, will survive, but as with anemones may pose a feeding problem. The feather worms need very small organisms such as newly hatched brine shrimp, so if the aquarist wishes to hatch them, he will have a source

The file shell filters particles from aquarium water and can move around by rapidly snapping its shells together. *Courtesy, William M. Stephens*

of food for them. Like anemones, they may feed on small, leftover particles of food that fish do not eat. They must be carefully watched like all other organisms in the aquarium to see what they will eat and if they continue to survive. They should be acclimated slowly without chemical treatment and should be watched to see if they remain retracted in their tubes. If they do not come out after several days, remove them and smell them to see whether they have died. Before doing this, however, lightly touch any part of the worm that might be protruding from its tube to see if it retracts farther. In this case the worm will still be alive and can be left for another day or two before removal and examination.

Mollusks such as snails and clams will do well, but, again, feeding may be a problem. Some snails feed on live organisms or dead particles, both of which are scarce in aquariums set up as outlined here. The filter feeders such as clams strain their food from the water and also would find very little to eat in this kind of aquarium. Snails, in addition, present a risk lest they die and decompose within their shells. This may release decomposition materials that are poisonous to fish. Clams, on the other hand, remain slightly agape when they are healthy and feeding, but too large a gape may mean they are hungry or dead. The shells of mollusks should be scraped thoroughly and washed with fresh water to remove foreign matter before they are introduced into aquariums. Snails should be acclimated slowly without chemicals, but little can be done with clams since they may remain closed for hours. Because of the potential problems with mollusks they are not recommended for the beginning aquarist.

Corals and gorgonians should be avoided by the aquarist unless he is willing to spend a lot of time trying to manipulate conditions in the aquarium to help them survive. Although they are quite different animals, they have very specific requirements for feeding that are beyond the means of most aquarists to provide. The major objection to their inclusion in marine aquariums is that feeding them and giving them the proper lighting might affect water quality and therefore the fish. Corals are kept by introducing certain chemicals into the water as well as very fine food organisms such as planktonic animals. The excess needed to get some food into them has its effect upon the environment of the aquarium and the shifts in equilibrium that occur may not be favorable.

This feather worm (attached to a sea squirt) strains small particles from water and makes an attractive addition to an aquarium. *Courtesy, William M. Stephens*

Section

II

ECOLOGY OF
MARINE FISHES IN
THEIR NATURAL
ENVIRONMENTS

9

Sea Habitats

INTRODUCTION

Keeping fish alive and healthy in an aquarium is a task requiring skill and understanding. A marine aquarium should be a small piece of ocean that fish find similar to their natural environment. Unfortunately, one cannot merely throw sand, coral and water together and provide the kind of conditions that a fish must have to survive. Merely taking these ingredients and confining them in a small space quickly results in changes in the water that soon are fatal to fish or other marine life that must live there. In the sea, small quantities of water are not confined. Water is continually mixing, and any given bucketful has much the same composition as any other with regard to a sufficient supply of oxygen, low amounts of contaminants and in many other ways. Continual mixing insures that areas that might contain too many waste products from organisms or which may be low in oxygen constantly mix with water that is richer in needed ingredients, but has less undesirable elements. The vast numbers of organisms that live in the oceans along with the currents, winds and other great forces exist together and influence each other in ways that keep the water in a prime condition for supporting life.

The task of the aquarist is clear, but difficult. He must keep the water in a prime condition as does the sea itself. His problem is that he does not possess the same biological and physical resources as does the sea. He must do as good a job, but his tools, of necessity, are different. And like it or not, he has another and difficult task to perform before he can use his tools. He needs to understand the processes in the sea that keep the natural environment healthy. With this background, he then can achieve a similar result in one small body of water he calls an aquarium.

One cannot simply put together a number of ingredients and have a healthy, functioning aquarium without some understanding of ecology, or how things work together. The marine aquarium is an excellent place to begin to understand this complex subject because it is a working ecological system. More importantly, it does not begin as such, so one has the advantage of working with a developing system. From the moment the aquarium is functioning, it begins to change and will continue to do so until it reaches a balance between the living and nonliving elements that comprise it.

This section is dedicated to the task of explaining how ecological factors in the sea work together to produce a healthy environment for marine life. With this knowledge to guide him, the aquarist will be better prepared to understand the changes that occur in his marine aquarium and how to deal with them using the tools at his command. With a knowledge of the sea and its processes to compare with his own system he will begin to understand the differences and what he has to do to compensate for them.

Few aquarists have much conception of the natural environment of tropical marine fishes. Most everyone has heard of coral reefs and of the warm, clear waters that bathe them, but the actual concept of the environment is obscure. The question of "why" this environment is so benign that it permits myriads of colorful and odd marine fishes to flourish is seldom asked. The general conditions that allow abundant life on coral reefs are known to scientists, although many of the details of how they work together still remain obscure. The purpose of this section is to discuss general conditions that make the marine environment healthy for the fish that live there and to show some of the relationships that are necessary for their survival.

CORAL REEF ENVIRONMENTS

Coral reef environments mostly are tropical and in general are submerged in clear marine waters. However, waters are not always crystal clear as popularly thought, but may become very turbid on occasion or may remain perpetually in various states of cloudiness. Degrees of cloudiness may be associated with particular areas; this is one factor that helps to determine which fish live there. The reasons for the cloudiness are another matter and will be discussed elsewhere in relation to their importance to marine life.

As the name implies, coral reefs are composed largely of corals. However, the corals are not always the exotic, branching underwater trees so often thought of as making up the bulk of such a reef. In many cases, they are lumps of calcium that are mostly dead except for a thin veneer of living animal material that is sculpted in designs varying from brainlike squiggles to a pincushion appearance. Their sizes are also vastly different with some as small as marbles and some as large as automobiles. Many areas of

The coral reef as envisoned by most people. Such profusion of coral is only a small part of many reefs and is nonexistent on others.

bottom may be covered by dead corals that are no more than rocks after the animals that composed them have died. As with everything that enters the marine world, and remains there, they are overgrown with "scumlike" marine plants and animals that use them as a place to anchor, expand and propagate.

The places where corals have yielded to the pressures of their environment and died are important for many reasons. One of these is that they permit the establishment of many other kinds of marine life which can gain a foothold in a dense jungle where it seems that every object is some form of life. Even the most minute piece of bottom can become a speck for conquest by tiny larvae of marine animals that blossom into branching treelike structures, whips or fans, tubes and other shapes that may bend and sway with the passage of water. Such tiny beginnings also give rise to rubbery sponges that punctuate a bottom with strings or globes or cylinders of bright colors. The flowery anemones and blossomlike worms also have such origins and colonize the "dead spots" to add to the profusion of life that forms the habitat of fish on coral reefs.

The corals, gorgonians, sponges, algae and other marine life that comprise coral reefs play a fundamental role in the lives of fish that live among them. They provide shelter which is basic for their survival. When predatory animals threaten, fish have places to hide among the branches of coral or in holes provided by spaces between the other growths on the bottom. If suitable nooks and crannies are not available, the bottom growth at least provides objects between and among which fish can dodge the approach of an enemy. Although they are quick, most coral reef fish that live among objects on the bottom are not accustomed to swimming fast for long distances as are many of the fish that hunt them; thus, they usually are found not far from shelter.

Hiding from predators is an obvious function of the shelter provided by fixed marine growths. However, shelter is also necessary from currents and surge that sweep many reefs with great force. Fish cannot swim for long periods of time against strong currents and remain in the same location because of excess demands on their energy reserves. The presence of corals and other marine growths protruding above the bottom slows the flow of water even though it may race past not far above it. Fishes that feed on drifting plankton regulate their distance above the bottom depending on how fast currents and surge are flowing. When water movement becomes too fast, they hover close to the bottom in eddies behind objects or take cover in holes where they sometimes can escape it completely. Surge is a greater problem for fish because its back-and-forth motion throws them against the objects in which they seek refuge and injures them. It is not surprising, therefore, that relatively few fish are found where there is surge. The continual swimming that fish must do in their natural environment in response to current helps keep them vigorous and in a healthy condition.

FEATURES OF HARD BOTTOM

The arrangement of corals and other marine growths on the bottom provides different kinds of habitats and shelter in addition to that which their shapes offer. Coral rock often covers the bottom over many acres or it may occur merely as patches interspersed in sandy or silt-laden areas. In places, it may be broken up to form rocks or boulders or may have edges that drop a few inches or many feet to form underwater shelfs or cliffs. Sometimes, the edges of such a coral outcrop, as hard bottom sometimes is called, may form a large hole with a sandy bottom or may run parallel to others forming a chasm. Edges are usually perforated with holes a fraction of an inch in size or they may be large enough to admit a man. In some instances, edges are undercut forming a long continuous overhang or ledge that also may be punctuated with caves that extend far under the coral shelf.

The globelike and branching corals, the gorgonians, sponges, algae and other growths on the bottom provide additional kinds of habitats and shelter. They may grow as single units, in small clumps or may cover the bottom in dense beds. Sometimes, these animal and plant colonies may be intermingled in bewildering assortments of shapes, sizes and colors. These different features provide varying habitats and, therefore, attract different kinds of fish. If the various animals and plants grow near crev-

Luxuriant growth that nonetheless has few associated fish. *Courtesy, James W. La Tourrette*

ices, caves or other such features, they may become better or worse places to live depending on the circumstances. For instance, a nearby crevice may be used as a home by some predatory species that would be well placed to catch other fish living nearby. A nearby crevice not so occupied, however, may offer an additional place for a fish to hide when danger threatens.

There are other features of the bottom and its growths that also are responsible for making a good habitat for certain species. Small holes or pieces of coral can only be entered by small fish and so are not attractive to larger species. The number of holes present also may limit the number of fish that can take cover.

The behavior of particular species goes hand in hand with how many fish can occupy a particular hole or

Vase sponge on type of bottom often associated with reef fishes. *Courtesy, James W. La Tourrette*

group of holes or crevices. Many species such as the bicolor damselfish, beau gregory and angelfish will not permit other fish to come close to them. Species with aggressive characteristics, therefore, are not found close together, even though there may be many suitable holes or crevices within a few inches or feet of each other. The blue reeffish and three-spot damselfish, on the other hand, will tolerate individuals of their own species and a single coral head may contain scores of them. Even here, however, their behavior is important, since they spend most of their time away from their coral head feeding and are more widely spaced so that aggressive tendencies are not aggravated.

Smaller shelter may accumulate more fish than usual when there are few other refuges available. Isolated coral

heads located in the midst of sandy areas or on low, flat
bottom often provide shelter for a number of different
species since there is no other cover available.

Because there are more holes and interstices available,
larger clumps of coral, jumbles of rocks or areas of
bottom perforated with holes generally accumulate more
fishes. Such places offer various-sized holes that often
interconnect providing a variety of shelter. These places
often are frequented by large numbers of different species
as well as different-sized individuals. Such accumulations
may represent complete little communities which include
the small colorful fish seen in aquariums as well as
larger predatory species that eat them. When some of
these predators become active, the smaller prey species
can reach shelter in an instant. But, when they blunder

Isolated coral head sheltering many reef fishes.

into range of the predators that lie quietly among them, there is little chance of escape from the lightning gulp that entraps them.

A bottom on which good shelter is located can be a poor habitat if it is located where water movement is strong. Areas of strong surge are inhabited only by species of reef fishes that are adapted to withstand this condition. Species such as jewelfish and gobies can be found in such locations, in part, at least, because they are ruggedly built and remain close to the bottom where they find shelter from the main force of the water. Some blennies and gobies lie on the bottom in holes and crevices where they are even more protected. On the other hand, some species of surgeonfish may inhabit turbulent areas where they simply drift with the surge rather than try to swim against it. They scrape their food from the bottom between surges during periods when the water is quieter. Turbulent areas, however, in spite of ample cover, do not generally have a large number of species associated with them.

Areas of sufficient cover that are located where there is a weak flow of water in some cases tend to have relatively few species of fish. Many small reef fishes depend on water flow to bring them the plankton on which they feed. With a constant flow of food, they do not have to move far from shelter and, therefore, can remain closer to their source of protection. When current is absent, the food supply of fish that depend on plankton essentially is cut off and they cannot survive well.

Slowly flowing water can have other consequences that restrict the distribution of fish. As water speed decreases, the often large volumes of sediment that it carries settles onto the bottom. The constant rain of sediment builds up on the bottom and chokes out much of the marine life that might otherwise grow there. The down current sides of large rock masses also may be subject to this kind of action and fish tend to avoid such places. Down current sides of rocks are less populated by fish that feed on plankton, since they congregate on the up current side to catch this food where it first enters their area. Although currents and surge present problems for fish, they are beneficial in many areas because they occur periodically and sweep away silt that builds up during calm periods and that otherwise would eventually clog the bottom.

Whether or not depth of water itself is a factor that limits the distribution of fish is difficult to answer. At least in shallow waters, the increase in pressure encountered over a change in depth from the surface to 100 or 200 feet probably has little effect on the normal bodily processes of fish. However, ecological conditions may be vastly different in shallow and deeper waters. Different kinds of cover exist at different depths in some localities

Shallow water reef area inhabited by a relatively few, hardier species of fish. *Courtesy, James W. La Tourrette*

because some of the attached marine life such as algae, corals and gorgonians do live at various depths. One of the most striking differences with depth is the general absence of surge in deeper waters. Surge activity usually is generated by waves on the surface and only extends for a limited distance beneath them. The presence of current in either shallow or deep water probably does not bother fish, since it flows only from one direction and they do not continually have to reverse direction to remain near their shelter.

SANDY HABITATS

The foregoing remarks have dealt with features of what is commonly called hard bottom. Sand is also found in the coral reef habitat either interspersed among coral or forming large areas by itself. There are far fewer species of fish associated with sandy habitats and most of them occur in sandy areas which contain some rocks or stones. Fish in sandy areas have the problem of finding suitable shelter just as do those that inhabit areas of hard bottom. Shelter is so scarce in sandy areas that relatively few species are able to exist there. Many fish such as some wrasses, the sand tilefish and flounders either bury themselves in an instant when attacked, or dive into holes they have dug. Shifting sand presents the worst problem because it sifts into burrows and fills them up. Whereas some species can live on bottom composed of sand and stones, few live on sand alone.

There are other species that are part-time users of sand as a place to feed. Because of their flat shape and ability to blend almost perfectly with their surroundings, flounders may lie in wait for smaller prey passing over sand.

Some grunts and snappers also feed over sand, but usually only under cover of darkness when the fishes that prey on them are inactive.

INTERTIDAL HABITATS

Another kind of habitat is found in the intertidal area which is covered by water during high tides, but is exposed to air when the water recedes. Species of blennies, gobies, some damselfish and others live in pools where they hide under rocks after the water level has dropped. When the water again returns, they become more active swimming around feeding and engaging in other activities.

Butterfly, squirrel and surgeon fish face the current in their natural habitat. *Courtesy, William M. Stephens*

Besides permanent residents, tide pools are inhabited by the young of many species including damselfish and butterfly fish. These pools are a harsh habitat because of the presence of very strong surge and washing activity of water. Fish must be very active in order to remain in the strong thrash of water while feeding and performing other activities without being dashed against rocks or washed away. But when waves are small or when tides are at either their lowest or highest points, wave action may be considerably reduced and sometimes is absent. More tranquil conditions, however, often are balanced by severe action due to high waves which prevent many species from becoming established during milder periods. Exposure to high temperatures as the sun heats the pools and dilution of seawater by rains are other ecological factors that help to restrict numbers of species in the intertidal areas.

Large coral head with closely spaced branches offering good shelter for fishes.

OTHER HABITAT LIMITATIONS

Within the broad framework of habitat as outlined are many features that further limit locations where particular species of fish will be found. The sponges, corals, rocks and other growth each may provide different kinds of shapes and, therefore, different kinds of shelter. Corals offer a variety of spaces into which fish can dart to shelter. Some have branches that are close together, others are wide apart and some form plates that may overlap. The depth of the spaces between branches also may vary widely from less than an inch to several feet. Some species of damselfish, gobies, cardinal fish and others are found almost exclusively with some species of corals that provide a particular kind of habitat for them. Protection among the branches of coral is not complete since small predatory fish may stalk among them or wait within and some species such as pipefish are long and thin and dart into spaces after prey.

Sponges offer an even more restricted habitat. Some fish live in the canals through which certain species of sponges pass water from without. A number of species of fish are found here and are considered as being commensal, or living together with their larger animal hosts and nowhere else. The sponges offer them ideal protection from predators outside and even may provide them with food, since small organisms are swept into the sponges' system of canals by the stream of water that circulates through them.

ROCK SHELTERS

The largest numbers of species of fish hide in holes and crevices in rocks for shelter. Rocks and ledges and

Large, dead coral head (covered by soft coral) with good hiding places for fish. *Courtesy, James W. La Tourrette*

large, dead coral heads that are riddled with holes often harbor many fish that live relatively close together. On close inspection it is evident that there is an organization of species and individuals with the various irregularities presented by the system of holes. Some species of damselfish remain within a few feet of the surface of the complex and will dart among the rocks and shallow holes on their surfaces when frightened. Other damselfish remain closer to the surface spending considerable time swimming among the holes. Even more reclusive species such as young rock beauties, some hamlets and young angelfish seldom expose themselves to view while foraging for food among shelter. The big-eyed cardinal fish almost never are seen outside cavities and caves where they hover in dim light awaiting nightfall when they will leave their shelter to feed outside. Royal grammas frequent caves or the undersides of overhangs where they take refuge in holes just large enough for them to enter.

The candy-striped bass is one of the most secluded of fish and can be seen only by quietly peering into the innermost recesses of caves. Complexes where such a variety of fish are found usually are the size of an automobile and must include numerous holes of various sizes. These complexes usually comprise only small areas of reef. Many smaller coral heads and rocks with appropriate kinds of holes and cavities containing fewer species of fish often can be found scattered over a reef.

SHELTER AND FOOD

A fish's shelter is located in some relation to its source of food. As mentioned earlier, species that are "tied" rather closely to a place of shelter must have the appropriate food close at hand. Young butterfly fish, rock beauties, and angelfish roam over a small area picking at tiny crabs, shrimps, worms, sponges and other creatures that live among the growth and in the crevices on the bottom. Small fish that live within sponges must feed on the small organisms that enter with water the sponge draws in unless they leave their host to feed. Some gobies, scorpion fish and others may roam around within a coral head feeding on smaller fish or invertebrates they find there. Other species such as surgeonfish and wrasses spend most of their time roaming the bottom without any particular place they call home. However, species such as these may congregate to feed in the same areas as those fish that roam little and may return to a particular section of reef where they spend the night.

NIGHTFALL AND REEF FISHES

Nightfall is a time of great change among fish that live on reefs. Most of the kinds we are familiar with that live in the open by day seek shelter as night falls. The smaller ones enter holes or crevices where they spend the night lying on the bottom, propped up against rocks or quietly "fanning" in one spot. Whether fish actually sleep as we think of it is unknown, but it is likely since some species may be picked up and handled without showing signs of activity. When disturbed too forcibly, however, some species dash blindly away sometimes injuring themselves against objects on the bottom. Not all species tuck themselves into tight quarters for the night. Some parrot fish, goatfish and possibly others merely prop themselves among coral or rocks. With some species at least, there are adaptations that help to keep them from being preyed upon at night. A mucous "cocoon" forms around some parrot fish probably protecting them from the prying noses of moray eels and perhaps sharks, crabs or other animals that might eat them. Goatfish and other species change color at night, which probably helps them to blend better with surroundings that are readily visible to the keen eyes of night-roving predators.

10

Function of Color
in Fishes

The subject of function of colors in fish is complex.
Colors have not developed merely to make them attractive to people. Their significance is geared toward the
cold, hard facts of their survival. In addition to the protection of shelter offered by corals, holes and rocks, many
fish have colors that help them to blend with the background coloration of the kind of bottom on which they
live. In general, species such as goatfish, coronet fish,
trumpet fish and others become darker, lighter or develop patterns to match their surroundings as they
swim over the bottom. These color changes can occur so
quickly in some species (e.g., coronet fish and flounders) that they render the fish quite invisible in an
instant. Other changes that match the fish to its background may take a matter of minutes or longer to
develop. In other cases, vivid colors that to us are seemingly conspicuous really blend well with the background
in which a fish is normally found. Rock beauties, juvenile
angelfish and jewelfish do not stand out among the
bright patches of living corals and other marine growth
among which they are found.

Color is important to the lives of fish for other reasons. Many species of damselfish, for instance, employ it
during reproductive activities when they are mating.
Male fish actively court females by performing loops and
dives over and around a small space on the bottom they

have cleared (where females eventually will lay eggs). During this ceremony, their colors become more vivid and usually are different than when they are picking algae off the bottom or performing other activities. The male three-spot damselfish turns a powder-blue color while its close relative from Hawaii becomes brilliant white except for a black tail and head. The bicolor damselfish is white with a black head and tail during courtship whereas the sergeant major develops brilliant copper and blue colors. When courtship activities wane, fish change to their more frequent colors within a minute and remain that way until they again attempt to entice a female to lay eggs in the areas they have cleared.

Fish also undergo striking color changes when they become aggressive. Again, the damselfish assume colors quite different from those seen during courtship or feeding. The bicolor damselfish becomes dark gray and develops a white vertical bar near the tail. The blue chromis becomes an even more dazzling blue and being less restricted to a particular location than the bicolor, may chase another fish many yards while so colored. The head of the blue surgeonfish becomes pale white when it chases its own species.

Knowing a fish's color as well as its use permits one to know something about its mood. In addition to color changes during moods of aggression and mating, colors may change with "fear" or "curiosity." The head, forepart of the body and tail of the adult three-spot damselfish from Hawaii become jet black both when they are curious about some unfamiliar object and also when they are found in murky water where they always appear to be easily frightened. The blue chromis and sergeant major turn dark when frightened and may remain thus for hours if danger persists. Darkening of colors also may occur in fish that are sick and relatively inactive.

11

Biological and Physical Factors

So far, only the role of shelter as an important part of the environment of fishes has been mentioned. Other essential features of their environment that create a healthy place for them to live are biological and physical factors associated with the water. Fish usually present a vigorous and healthy appearance when observed in their natural environment. Movements are brisk as they feed, mate, chase each other and carry out other activities. Colors are vivid and fins are transparent and sharp edged. Fish retreat in a flash from whatever frightens them and bounce out again to resume their active lives after danger has passed. When feeding, they dart quickly from one particle of food to another. Their vigorous health and behavior are a reflection of the good quality of the water in which they live.

Good water quality in a fish's natural environment is a result of important events that occur there. In order to understand the importance of good water quality, it is necessary to know something about the factors that tend to make it inhospitable for animals that live in it. Some of these factors are associated with the animals and plants themselves, and others with nonbiological phenomena.

PHYSICAL FACTORS

Among the most important nonbiological factors that affect water quality are temperature and salinity. Some species of fishes can tolerate a wide range of salinities and temperatures whereas others die if exposed to small changes. In general, fishes that live in places such as estuaries, which are a middle ground between freshwater rivers and the sea, can live in water that is either quite fresh or salty. These areas may vary widely in temperature, and fishes that are found there consequently must tolerate higher as well as lower temperatures. Some species that live in estuaries, however, are not exposed to all of the extremes since they move up or down in the water or find locations where conditions are more moderate. Mollies and killifish are well-known for their abilities to tolerate estuarine conditions.

Nonbiological factors that create poor water quality also occur directly or indirectly through man's activities and are especially damaging in estuaries. Inflow of pesti-

Squirrelfish gets ready to dart into its hole at the approach of a diver. *Courtesy, William M. Stephens*

cides, plasticizers and other products can be concentrated by fish usually by eating food organisms that have first concentrated it in their bodies. Some of these materials also may enter fish through their gills and skin. If concentrations become too great, fish may die or may become so weakened that they are not hardy enough to survive the rigors of their natural environment. These foreign materials do not have to kill fish directly but may alter their temperature (and possibly other) tolerances so that they can no longer resist cold or heat normally.

Another condition that may result in poor water quality in the natural environment is the presence at times of heavy waves that churn bottom sediments that have lain undistrubed for long periods of time. Under these conditions, the water may become choked with parts of plants, animals and silt, and if it is dense enough, such material may clog the gills of fish and interfere with breathing. High concentrations of gasses such as hydrogen sulfide and other chemical decomposition products associated with a disturbed bottom are forms of natural pollution that adversely affect fish. The amount of oxygen in the water sometimes is reduced by heavy bottom stirring and fishes have been known to die from suffocation. Heavy bacterial action which further depletes oxygen often contributes to this type of destruction of fish. Even though amounts of deleterious substances may be relatively small, their combined effects may be harmful. Fish that live in enclosed, shallow bays and sounds are more likely to be exposed to such dangerous conditions associated with heavy wave action.

Relatively poor water quality also occurs under highly localized conditions. As mentioned with currents, water flow is slower near the bottom due to interference by rocks and other objects that cause drag. In crevices, holes and caves flow may be very slight although current is pre-

Jawfish live in holes where water is likely of poorer quality than outside. *Courtesy, Wometco Miami Seaquarium*

sent outside them. The burrows of tilefish, jawfish and other species that live in such places seldom may be subject to a complete change of water except through the motion of fish passing in and out. Small, isolated "cells" of water where there is little exchange with the outside are places where waste products may accumulate and depletion of oxygen may occur. They are essentially small pockets that are polluted to some degree or other depending on the amount of flushing that occurs and the amount of biological and other chemical changes that occur there. Fish that live for varying periods of time under such conditions, therefore, must be adapted to existing conditions of poorer water quality than those that spend most of their time out in the open water. It is accepted among ichthyologists that fish that live close to the bottom, in holes or in "muddy" areas are hardier than species that live off the bottom in areas where there is little accumulation of waste products.

WATER FLOW AND WASTE PRODUCTS

Biological factors that reduce water quality are concerned with living organisms. Living plants and animals eliminate waste products, many of which are harmful to themselves as well as to other organisms. It is essential, therefore, that waste products either be removed from the organism's presence or rendered harmless by some means. Both of these situations occur in the natural environment and details of their workings are complex. However, an examination of how and why they occur is of great importance, since life cannot exist without them.

Water flow is of fundamental importance for the removal of waste products in aquatic environments. This prevents the buildup of harmful concentrations of materials at sites where they are produced. The role of water in removing waste products and other harmful substances can be compared with the removal of polluted air by wind in land environments especially over large cities. The buildup of materials in holes and crevices in watery environments illustrates the need for moving water in waste disposal.

A subtle but important factor in keeping water clean in the natural environment is the great amount of water in the sea when compared to the area of the bottom. Even with all the profusion of life producing vast amounts of waste products on or near the bottom, there is a large quantity of water in which it can be diluted. If there was only enough water to barely cover the bottom of the sea, it is obvious that there would not be enough to dilute all the waste products produced which would build up to harmful proportions. The more water there is, then, in comparison to the amount of bottom, the better it is for living organisms.

The number of fish in comparison to the amount of

water works similarly. If there are few fish and a great quantity of water regardless of whether or not they were near the bottom, dilution of waste products will be great. If there is little water, but many fish, dilution will be less and waste will accumulate faster. As one can imagine, shallow estuarine areas and particularly those that are more completely enclosed are more vulnerable to concentrations of harmful substances because there is less water to dilute them in comparison with the relatively large area of the bottom with all its organisms as well as those swimming in the water.

Still another important mechanism in the sea that helps keep the water fit for living organisms is one that only recently has been recognized. Oddly enough, bubbles themselves have the function of exerting a scouring action which removes dissolved substances that are harmful to animals if they accumulate. These substances are mostly proteins that to a chemist are rather large molecules. When they come in contact with some surfaces, they adhere to them and, therefore, no longer are free in the water. They stick to the surfaces of bubbles as well as other objects and, since bubbles are formed in immense numbers by breaking waves, large molecules are removed in great quantities. When bubbles carrying these molecules on their surfaces churn around, they form froth which floats on the surface of the sea where it is harmless to animals swimming in the water from which it was removed.

REMOVAL OF WASTE PRODUCTS BY BACTERIA

Even though moving water, dilution and bubble scavenging removes wastes, it is apparent that sooner or later a body of water even as large as the sea would become polluted if such products remained in the environment indefinitely. This disturbing possibility has been taken care of, however, by the origin through millions of years of organisms that are able to use waste products and that reduce or eliminate their harmful properties. These organisms, consisting mainly of species of bacteria, are microscopic in size and are tremendously abundant so that their combined activities can break down huge amounts of harmful materials. But what happens to the waste products produced by all the bacteria? Do they not build up in astronomical proportions and are they not harmful to life? The answers lie in the fact that waste products of the bacteria are used by other bacteria and also by different kinds of microscopic plants and animals. These plants and animals are eaten by even larger kinds of animals including fish. At this point we are back where we started with the waste products of fish and other organisms being used as food by bacteria. The plants and animals live together and depend upon each other for food in a situation that has no beginning and no end. Each organism, both plant and animal, is a middleman that uses certain materials and then is itself used by others. This endless chain of utilization, called a cycle, provides that only a certain amount of any material is usually present in a particular form at a particular time. Viewed in this light, there is no such thing as a waste product since the waste of one organism is really the fuel for another. The idea of waste, however, is useful when materials occur in proportions that might be harmful to organisms. In this case, we can call a buildup of materials that interfere with life in some way pollution.

The important materials that concern us with the cycle we have just seen involve the element nitrogen. Waste products such as albumins and amines that are eliminated by animals into the water or occur there as uneaten parts of plants and animals are attacked and used as food by bacteria. Some bacterial action releases into water the nitrogenous compound ammonia. This material is highly poisonous to most living organisms and actually is used as a food by other kinds of bacteria. When bacteria utilize ammonia, they in turn release other nitrogen compounds called nitrites. Other species attack the nitrite and in turn produce nitrogen-containing compounds called nitrates. At this point, plants, both microscopic and larger, utilize the nitrates which are used along with other compounds to make more plants. Each of the nitrogen compounds, the ammonia, nitrites and nitrates are succeedingly less poisonous with the latter having the least harmful effects.

The bacteria that are chiefly responsible for elimination or changing the composition of dissolved waste products exist in great numbers on the surfaces of practically anything and are especially active on small particles which they eventually may consume. Many particles, however, including feces and parts of plants and animals are eaten by various animals and thus are removed from the environment as a source of pollution. Marine animals such as clams and tunicates draw a current of water through a netlike structure within them on which particles distinguished as food are retained and eaten. Some worms, brittle stars and other organisms extend a netlike apparatus into the water and snare particles that float past them. Other animals such as the flowerlike anemones and hydroids and some corals have microscopic darts that discharge in volleys to catch and hold small animals or particles that strike them whereas other corals use slime for catching food. These types of marine animals entrap living as well as nonliving particles and may eat different proportions of foods depending on a number of circumstances such as preference and availability.

The foregoing activities of marine organisms remove

waste particles and small food animals that drift above as well as near the bottom. Enormous numbers of particles, of course, settle on the bottom or are deposited there by organisms. That part of this material that is usable becomes the food for numerous groups of animals that live there and search for it by using various kinds of behavioral activities to detect and capture it. Among the most commonly known bottom living scavengers are crabs and shrimps that sense food with their legs and other structures among the particles and growth that cover the bottom. Particles may come to rest anywhere and different species of these animals are adapted to live and to search for food among rocks, in the open sand or hard bottom and some even among the branches of upright growths. Since they are free to move around, they clean up small patches of bottom or the growth on which they are living. Other smaller free living animals such as shrimps and the shrimplike amphipods also aid in removing waste particles from among the smaller nooks and crannies. The list of marine animals that scour the bottom for the waste that is their food is much longer and includes brittle stars and some urchins that bore through the bottom, feeding as they go. When one considers the great numbers of marine animals that utilize partially or exclusively the waste products and fragments of others one can visualize the vast, busy clean-up program that nature has developed for keeping the environment clean for all.

Seawater also is kept healthy for animals because a relatively constant pH is maintained. Water is considered to be either acid or nonacid (basic) and the term pH is used to describe these conditions. A pH of 7.0 arbitrarily is considered to be the dividing line between acid and basic. Offshore seawater usually has a pH of about 8.2 whereas that near some shores varies somewhat because it is affected by drainage from nearby land and other factors. Many of the physiological reactions that keep animals alive and healthy are related to pH in complex ways making it important for them to live in waters of the proper pH. Mechanisms involving carbon dioxide, water, and calcium in the form of particles such as sand operate together in a system that assures that seawater will have the proper pH. The mechanisms involve the relative abundance of hydrogen, carbonate and bicarbonate ions, the dissolving and formation of minerals and other processes. The metabolic activities of living organisms, temperature and carbon dioxide from the atmosphere also affect pH and therefore are part of the system that regulates it. The basic chemistry that leads to changes in pH in salt water is understood and is the same there as in the aquarium.

12

Fish Behavior

The foregoing discussion points out major ecological factors that keep the environment of reef fishes healthy. There are other events in the environment that are important to the well-being of fish and, therefore, are important to their survival. These events concern the behavior of fish which has changed through the ages to meet changes in their environment. Just as claws, fins, teeth, and nets provide animals with the tools for living in their environment, their behavior provides them with the mechanisms by which they correctly use the tools for survival. As one might expect, much behavior is in one way or another related to obtaining food, escaping enemies and assuring reproduction.

OBTAINING FOOD—GENERAL INFORMATION

Feeding behavior of fish varies widely not only between species, but also with the size of the individual. In general, reef fish communities are organized from the standpoint of feeding behavior as follows: there is a large grouping of many species of fish that live close to the

bottom where they spend most of their lives within a
radius of 10 or 20 feet of a particular spot. Some of these
species feed almost totally on the bottom where they pick
small animals, plants or both from the congestion of life
found there. Others feed almost exclusively a short distance above the bottom where they dart around snapping
up small drifting animals or plants that float past. Feeding above or on the bottom, however, does not restrict
most species from occasionally switching to feed in one or
the other location for a time.

A close look at an aggregation of fish feeding above
the bottom reveals interesting and important facets of
their lives. Aggregations have a definite organization that
results from an interplay between ecological factors such
as predation and behavior. In most species, fish that
feed farthest from the refuge are the largest. The smaller
the individual, the closer to the refuge it feeds with the
smallest often remaining within the confines of its shelter.
Probably because they are closer to the bottom, smaller
fish of some species spend a lot of time feeding there
instead of up in the water where adults are located. The
feeding organization, therefore, is such that the small,
weaker swimmers are close to the bottom where they can
hide quickly and the larger, stronger ones, although farther away, also can reach it fast because of their greater
speed.

Another important aspect of feeding aggregations is the
spacing of individuals. Although fish may momentarily
come quite close to each other as they dart around after
food, they usually remain some distance apart. This spacing is maintained by natural aggressive tendencies since
fish will attack others at times when they come too close.
Often, all that is needed is for one fish to "aim" itself at
another and briefly rush at it to induce flight. If the fish
does not flee, the attacker may dash faster and briefly

chase the other. Most attacks are split-second affairs and may go unnoticed if one is not watching closely. Attacks by large fish on small ones may be another mechanism that tends to keep smaller individuals closer to shelter. When a feeding aggregation is threatened, fish usually draw close together, the mutual danger reducing tendencies toward aggression.

Feeding aggregations are often comprised of more than one species, the individuals of which intermingle. Species of damselfish are frequently found together and wrasses, gobies and other fish also may be included. Aggressive clashes occur between the species, but usually are less frequent than among individuals of the same species. Occasionally, attacks both between species and among the same species are sustained and an individual may be chased many yards.

Among fish that pick small organisms from the bottom, spacing is even more critical for preventing aggressive conflicts. Damselfish and young angelfish, for instance, are more highly territorial than species that swim freely above the bottom probably because they are in contact with objects to which they form "attachments." Objects on the bottom can be used accurately to define boundaries although "normal" spacing requirements and other behavioral problems may be involved in aggressive territorial behavior. With defined territories, bottom-feeding fish in general tend to be more widely dispersed than those feeding above the bottom so they do not come into as close contact as the latter. Size, again, also is a factor since small fish provoke fewer and less sustained attacks from larger individuals than those more equally matched in size.

Aggression may be more or less intense, probably imposing greater or lesser restrictions to feeding on the bottom. During the reproductive season aggression

Camouflaged shrimp lives among poisonous spines of a sea urchin which it is constructed to resemble. *Courtesy, William M. Stephens*

becomes more intense among males of some species which are quicker to chase another fish than usual. During this period attacks also tend to reach out farther into areas where others are usually tolerated. Among at least some species that lay eggs on the bottom that are guarded by a male, attacks become more frequent and intense when eggs are present.

Although many species of fish feed on a wide variety of organisms, some have more narrow diets. Adult angelfish of some species, for instance, feed on sponges they scrape from the bottom. Parrot fish in many cases feed almost exclusively on algae they scrape from the bottom although some also feed on corals. Butterfly fish are known to feed on coral animals which they pull out one at a time from the tiny holes in which they live. Feeding habits of fish in their natural environments in most cases is complex because of individual tastes, different kinds of food that are available at different times, changing tastes with size and many other factors.

Fish often do not merely pounce upon and snap up

potential food. The plankton feeders sometimes dart at an object and then stop to inspect it before grabbing it. Even after grabbing something, they may hesitate a few moments apparently tasting it and then may spit it out only to grab it again and repeat the process. Even the larger predatory fish sort out prey by letting larger individuals pass unmolested while quickly seizing smaller fishes they can swallow.

Predatory fish do not feed as often as those fish that eat small organisms from the plankton or the bottom. One main type of predator—including scorpionfish and frog fish—mostly catches prey that remain on the bottom or return there after feeding in the water above. Their general mode of hunting is to move quietly from one spot to another in search of prey. They approach as close as possible and then lie quietly and inconspicuously until a victim swims into range of a fast gulp. Basses and groupers slink from one hole to another or to the bases of rocks and other objects where they also wait for smaller fish to approach. They may dart quickly over a short distance to grab their victim or may suck it into their mouths almost without moving if the latter approaches closely enough. Although many of them hunt more actively early in the morning or just before dark, they are great opportunists and will feed whenever they have a chance. They take advantage of disturbances in the marine community and sometimes are rewarded with a meal. The rummaging around of fish as they feed often cause other fish or organisms such as crabs and shrimp to flee literally into the jaws of waiting predators. The possibility of "cashing in" on the efforts of others must be profitable as one can see predatory species moving toward places where disturbances are occurring. Also it is not unusual to see groupers, pipefish and other predatory species swimming side by side with larger fish that are not recognized as predators by smaller species. Smaller fish often allow lumbering parrot fish and large wrasses to come close to them at which time the predator, shielded by the body of the larger fish, dashes out and makes its capture.

Preoccupation with reproductive activities also affords an opportunity for predators to gain a meal. Many of the small damselfish gyrate in a series of loops or twists as they attempt to entice females to the "nest" site they have prepared. During these displays males apparently are not as wary, their attention being focused on the females and at such times they are caught by the flashing attack of a predator.

The long, thin coronet and trumpet fish are bizarre groups that skulk among growths on the bottom in search of prey. The trumpet fish may drift head down letting the motion of the water rock them back and forth, giving them a most unfishlike appearance. When a small fish or crab is seen they "aim" toward it and approach stealthily with undetectable movements of their small, colorless fins. When seen head on by prey, they almost disappear because they are so thin and their distance is probably difficult to judge until it is too late. Their coloring is that of their surroundings, adding to their effectiveness as predators. In turn, when they are stalked, they may retreat among corals or gorgonians where their sticklike bodies resemble just another branch.

In addition to groupers, basses, hawkfish, scorpion fish and other predators that live on the bottom are those that swim more actively above it. Among these are the yellow tail snappers and the jacks. They are more streamlined and swim faster than fish that live on the bottom. They often gather in schools which roam over reefs in search of other fish on which they prey. Schooling has advantages for these kinds of predators that

Lone coronet fish drifts vertically among coral in search of prey.
Courtesy, Wometco Miami Seaquarium

usually catch their prey by chasing them. When jacks, for
instance, encounter a group of smaller fish and begin to
chase them, the latter often dart away from one pursuer
only to blunder into the path of another which catches it.
If the prey fish form into a tight school, the attack of a
number of predators is more likely to pry loose some
individuals which again are subject to attack from different directions. All of the attacking fish might not catch a
meal during every encounter, but on the average each
individual will eventually catch its share of the food that
is available over a period of time.

Community behavior is one of great activity. In the
early morning shortly after dawn, fish that are active
during the day leave the crevices and caves where they
spent the night and begin to feed. This is a time of
intense feeding since most of the day fish have not fed
at night and hunger is probably keen. In the increasing
light, clusters of plankton feeders become conspicuous as
they hover in umbrella formations above their particular
coral head or other shelter. The large, bolder individuals
dash about after food farther away from the shelter than
the smaller ones and in shallow water they may form a

curtain of fish that reaches to the surface. On some reefs, large sergeant majors and three-spot damselfish may form groups that roam around over some hundreds of feet.

The abundant, colorful wrasses may be part-time feeders on plankton taking their stations along with fish that are up and around in the water full time. Wrasses are roamers that wander among the clutter of growth on the bottom seeking food. At one moment, they hover in the current and then are off across the bottom again. They cluster around objects that seem to interest them as likely sources of food and are quick to seize the small crabs, worms and other organisms they eat. Like larger predators, they are opportunists and quickly gather at the site of any disturbance. They follow parrot fish, surgeonfish, goatfish and others that disturb the bottom while feeding and quickly snap up the small organisms that seek to escape these intrusions into their homes.

The parrot and surgeonfish also wander over the bottom in groups like the wrasses. Their movements add

School of wrasses inspecting source of potential food. *Courtesy, James W. La Tourrette*

Parrot fish en route to grazing area. *Courtesy, Wometco Miami Seaquarium*

much color and activity to the marine community as they flap along on large winglike pectoral fins. Stopping here and there they scrape the algae and coral from the bottom with large buck teeth. Chisellike gouges on the bottom and on the sides of rocks and coral are unmistakable signs of their passing. The loud rasping they make as they feed identifies their presence even when they are too far away to see. Like the wrasses and other bottom roamers, they often blunder into trouble when they happen into a territory guarded by a small but fierce damselfish. The ensuing fight is all one-sided and is over quickly with the speedy damselfish everywhere at once nipping fins, tail, sides, bottom and any part of the intruder that does not clear the area immediately. These vicious attacks, often accompanied by a sharp popping noise, are a powerful offense as anyone can testify who has seen a parrot fish a hundred times the size of a damselfish shudder as though hit by a club after one fierce bite. Even the large groupers that feed on the damselfish are not immune. The damselfish are even more crafty when attacking so formidable an intruder. After waiting for their large, slow target to pass, they flash from cover, deliver a lightning bite on the tip of the passing tail and streak for cover again. The larger fish cannot possibly turn in time to catch its antagonist and must be content to speed up and be on its way.

The less common butterfly fish and larger angelfish also weave their way among the growths and other fish in the community. Their disklike shapes add a different look to the community that is dominated by the more fish-like shapes of most of the inhabitants. Often found in pairs, they drift among the corals, gorgonians and other growths examining them for food. The smaller butterfly fish pick daintily at the tiny crustaceans and coral animals whereas the more robust angelfish crunch at the growths much as do the parrot and surgeonfish. On occasion, the butterfly fish like many others turn to face the current and share in the crop of plankton that drifts above the reef. The undersides of a floating jellyfish may even be a source of food showing how wide may be the diet of some fish when the opportunity for a meal is presented.

Among the less numerous fish in the reef community are an assortment of species including the basses, hinds and hamlets. Their presence is less noticeable than the active plankton feeders as they wait quietly in one spot ready for the quick dash that nets them a meal. Jawfish dip and bob about close to the bottom picking out the food they want from the plankton. When a dangerous fish approaches slowly, they back tail first into the holes they have excavated in the bottom. If they are frightened sud-

Angel and butterfly fish hover around coral offering them a potential source of food. *Courtesy, James W. La Tourrette*

denly, they dive head first into their burrows with great speed. Royal grammas in caves live upside-down lives keeping their bellies toward the ceiling while catching small organisms, chasing each other and moving around in general. The young of many species are very reclusive remaining close to holes and crevices. Being timid, they are gone from sight at the first sign of unusual activity. Many of the night-roving species such as cardinal fish rarely are seen at all unless one peers into the seclusion of their caves. Grunts that feed at night may be seen in schools that hang quietly in one spot waiting for the return of darkness.

The buzz of activity among the members of the fish community may slow toward afternoon especially if currents that bring plankton are absent. As fish move closer to the bottom they lose interest in feeding on plankton and begin to explore and pick at algae and other growths on the bottom. During this time, the fish that were more widely spaced and preoccupied with feeding now congregate more closely. When they become crowded in this way, aggression increases and chases are more common.

The generally lethargic activity may continue until

dark if current remains absent. If current begins to flow, however, the community springs to life and vigorous feeding activity again begins. The presence of food borne by currents is a strong influence that obviously is important to at least some marine fish communities. Feeding formations slowly sink closer to the bottom as darkness approaches and fish finally disappear into their shelters by the time it is dark.

REACTION TO PREDATORY FISHES

The fish community as a whole reacts in two main ways to the approach of predatory fish. Those nearest to slowly approaching predators swim at moderate speeds toward the bottom before they are approached too closely. Other fish in the community follow this lead as predators continue into the community. While those being approached are swimming downward toward shelter, those that have been passed leave cover and swim upward away from the bottom again. The appearance is that of a wave passing through the fish community as numbers of fish sink down in front of a predator and then flow up again behind it.

If predators remain close, fish nearest them remain close to shelter until they have moved on. If predators begin to chase smaller fish or approach swimming fast, all the fish dash for the bottom at once and disappear from sight. At times, fast-swimming jacks and other swift-schooling predators separate and flash back and forth across the community at high speed creating great confusion among the smaller individuals. Panic sets in and smaller fish may be caught as they dart among the growths on the bottom. The speed of the attack frequently is so great that small fishes swimming above the bottom are cut off from their only refuge as they dive toward it. After the community has been "beat up" in such a manner the smaller fish are quite shy and it is a while before they venture forth from shelter to resume feeding.

The foregoing description of the lives of fish on reefs is quite general and does not always apply to all fish. There are many thousands of species of fish living on reefs, no two of which are exactly the same. The various features of habitats and environments dealt with in this section can be found mixed in different proportions, although some reefs can be remarkably similar. The behavior of fish as other animals reflect the set of environmental conditions that are found in their locality. On some reefs, for instance, fish are shy because water is turbid and they cannot see the approach of a predator until it is close at hand. Under these conditions, fish remain close to shelter most of the time. Conversely, when fish can see a long distance in clear water, they swim much farther from shelter partially, at least, because they can see approaching danger at a distance. Some reefs have greater numbers of predators than others and here, too, fish in a community are more shy since they are attacked or approached more frequently. A community may be composed of only a few or many species depending on how many different kinds of habitats comprise it. It is not surprising that fish of the same species act differently in some ways depending on where they live.

With all of the great forces that act in the sea and the vast complex of marine life that interacts with them, one easily can get the impression that it is all a great mixture of these ingredients. Nothing could be further from the truth. Life in the sea, as everywhere on earth, is well ordered. Individual shrimps, crabs, fish and other organisms often live out their lives on the bottom without moving more than a few yards from where they settle after a planktonic life of drifting with ocean currents. When viewed in this light, life on the bottom of the sea or at least on reefs, with some qualifications, actually is composed of various-sized, balanced aquariums with many characteristics that are similar to the ones we attempt to keep in our homes and laboratories.

The features of the bottom mentioned earlier, including the attached marine life, have a lot to do with producing this aquarium effect. Since different kinds of animals require different kinds of habitats, they concentrate in places with which they are compatible. For instance, some of the slow, brightly colored fishes must remain near shelter into which they quickly can dart when danger threatens and which provides a background of similar coloration into which they blend. This kind of habitat is provided by a bottom strewn with rocks, coral and other objects which offer nooks and crannies with matching colors. Dull-colored, lumpy-appearing fishes that do not move much must remain on a bottom that contains objects that are irregular in shape and contains matching colors. Either of the types of fish mentioned would stand out vividly if found over sand or even a hard, flat bottom. We can begin to see with these examples why many different species remain in one location for most of their lives. To move from one location to another often requires migration across sand or otherwise bare bottom where the fish is vulnerable to predation. The distance between the proper kind of habitat for a species, therefore, is a prime reason why many fish tend to remain in locations they find when young. If the distances are short, more movement from one location to another can occur. If they are long, individuals remain quite isolated for their whole lives. The author has seen an extreme case of the latter situation in the Marshall Islands of the Pacific

Ocean where young and adults of three species of damsel-fish were living together in one coral head. The isolation in a large patch of sand was so complete that adults of all three species were spawning in and around the coral.

Major differences between these natural aquariums and the kind that people keep occur because the former are not isolated from some of the features of the environment. Water, of course, flows past a colony of fish that otherwise are isolated from other groups and some species of larger, fast-swimming fish come and go. As we have seen, flowing water removes and dilutes waste products while replenishing the area with cleaner water that has been processed by the sea itself as well as by living organisms. It also brings food and new inhabitants to the location in the form of tiny planktonic organisms that will settle on the bottom and grow into new replacements for the colony. The natural daylight provides energy needed to make the essential plants grow and to warm the waters so life can function.

We now begin to see some of the ingredients that the aquarist must provide for his closed system. He must keep the water clean and healthy for his fish, invertebrates and plants and must provide them with food. He must provide the gadgets that substitute for natural processes that keep the water healthy and must manipulate living organisms themselves to do part of the job while not contributing an excess of their own waste products. In short, he must create an ecological complex that is balanced like that of his larger rival, the sea. Finally, it should be apparent that like the natural aquariums in the sea, our closed aquarium systems are not really closed at all. We must put into them the light, the food, the temperature, and we must even replenish the organisms themselves when they have been removed for one reason or another.

13

The Advanced Aquarist

The instructions and advice given the beginning aquarist should be followed as closely as possible because he does not yet have a "feel" for what he is doing. The concept of a "feel" or "green thumb" as it might be called, is not a mystical insight. Rather, it results from an ability to recognize signs of change, and that particular adjustments will produce predictable changes in a certain length of time. Obviously, much experience is needed to gain these perspectives. To recognize a change in the behavior of a fish, one must be familiar with its "normal" activities. To be relatively confident that installing a new wooden air breaker in a protein skimmer will eliminate signs of stress in fish requires that one can recognize an inefficient skimmer as well as the probability that it is the most likely explanation for recognized trouble. And it helps to have had such trouble previously and to have noted that it was corrected by a similar procedure. These are only a few illustrations that might help to show how experience will aid in maintaining a marine aquarium.

After the aquarist has the experience necessary to manipulate confidently the conditions in his aquarium, he is in a position to take liberties that would be disastrous for the beginner. Manipulating conditions in the aquarium makes it possible to keep more difficult marine organisms, thus giving the aquarist the opportunity to play with infinite variations in the life in his aquarium. Probably, the most exciting introductions he can make are the varieties of nonfish life which include invertebrate animals and plants. Among these are living algae that have many pleasing forms. Some of these growths may appear feathery, wheel shaped or occur in grapelike clusters, whereas others are more conventional bush types. Their colors range through green, brown, red and even blend into blue green and other hues.

Among the animals are forms such as feather worms, clams, corals and anemones that have intricate shapes, designs and colors. They are stationary (except anemones and some clams), but may move to some extent even though attached. The lightning withdrawal of a feather worm into its tube, for instance, is fascinating to watch.

The sea stars and urchins, various crabs, worms and many other invertebrates move around burrowing, searching for food and performing other activities. Many people find them more interesting to watch than fish. These animals, like algae, come in a great variety of shapes and colors that never seem to end. The sights of brittle stars skittering along on spike-studded "arms" or supple worms "boring" their way through sand along the glass side of an aquarium are awe inspiring. Many people devote their aquariums only to such forms of life.

It would be difficult to discuss the procedures for keeping all the various kinds of marine organisms in aquariums. Even within a group of animals, such a thing as food requirements may vary considerably. Some sea stars, for instance, eat living prey (e.g., clams) whereas others feed on nonliving material. Some mollusks also do this and some may strain water for food whereas others seek it by moving around.

As with fish, different invertebrates vary in their adaptability to aquarium life in respect to how well they can tolerate water conditions, lighting, etc. Some starfish, worms and crabs can live in water lethal to fish, although a condition such as low oxygen can kill most forms of life.

Some generalizations can be made to help the individual who wishes to try his hand at widening the scope of marine life in his aquarium. With plants he should remember that lighting is very important. Some species such as green algae do well with strong direct light whereas red algae in general are favored by more reduced illumination. Placing them under the arms of coral or in other shaded portions of an aquarium will help if bright light happens to be present. Plants should be observed to see if dead or dying parts are present so that future dieback can be recognized. No particular feeding of plants seems to be necessary, especially if a few fish or invertebrate animals are present.

Light does not seem to be particularly important to most invertebrates in aquariums with the exception of anemones and corals that need it for algae contained within them. Many invertebrates need shelter, so coral, rocks or other cover should be present. Since feeding requirements vary, the diet of a particular species should be known before it is kept in captivity. This information can usually be obtained from pet or aquarium shops or from books dealing with aquarium and marine life.

Fragments, or even whole rocks containing attached marine animals and/or plants, make interesting additions to an aquarium. All manner of organisms attach themselves to rocks and it is not uncommon to have a dozen or more species present on one rock. On the other hand, rocks may be completely overgrown by small anemones, algae, soft corals, tunicates and other organisms. One advantage of introducing animals attached to rocks is that they are not injured since they do not have to be pried loose. A problem with such introductions, however, is that unnoticed organisms also might be placed in the aquarium. Often these are hidden in holes and may be out of view within the rock. A careful search sometimes detects their presence, especially if holes are lined indicating the presence of marine worms. The undersides of rocks often are encrusted with brightly colored patches of sponge and/or algae that might release toxic substances if they are damaged or killed. The aquarist should be aware of the presence of such organisms so he can either eliminate or care for them. Animals that die undetected in holes are a potential threat to other life in an aquarium, especially if their presence is undetected.

Placing overgrown rocks, algae and other organisms in an aquarium that has been set up with fish for only a few months can lead to trouble. An aquarium may not be fully stabilized in this period of time and feeding and other problems associated with new organisms may quickly alter the properties of the water and harm fish. Other organisms should be introduced one at a time or in small colonies and should be watched carefully to see that they are not sick or dying. Their food especially should be watched to see that it does not pollute the aquarium. Fish should be watched carefully for changes in behavior and appearance that might indicate deteriorating water quality and also to see how they respond to whatever is introduced. Aquariums that have been established for about six months or more are likely to be less affected by new introductions but should be watched just as closely.

Aquariums originally set up with invertebrates or large algae are less likely to be adversely influenced by introducing new organisms. Main problems seem to be concerned with compatibility of the organisms. Crabs might eat algae or other organisms and anemones can prey on crabs, worms or other animals that come in contact with them. It is wise to stay away from burrowing animals such as heart urchins or some snails (e.g., olive and auger shells) which may remain under sand even when sick or dying. An aquarium started with large algae and then populated after some months, with fish and/or invertebrates is usually most attractive and healthy.

The main thing to remember when keeping any organisms in an aquarium is that good water quality is still the most important consideration. Therefore, the basic setup and maintenance as outlined previously should be followed to insure good water quality. This involves everything from the proper lights and filters to care in feeding the occupants. With different organisms modifications must be made, of course. For instance, anemones require a lot of light (GroLux is good) and small pieces of shrimp, crab or other food of marine origin should be dropped on their tentacles to feed them. Filter feeders such as clams, feather worms and tunicates will thrive if newly hatched live brine shrimp are added to the aquarium for them to extract. All the while, however, thought must be given as to how these additions and manipulations to the aquarium are affecting it. The aquarist's previous experience will go far in helping him to determine this. Any modifications should be made without interfering with the normal procedures and apparatus that provide good water quality.

In spite of this cautious note, it nonetheless is possible to maintain an aquarium without the use of several pieces of equipment. Whether or not this can be done depends on the kind and numbers of organisms present. If a large number of animals (especially those that move around a lot) are present, it is probable there are not enough bacteria to process their wastes. Under these conditions, the protein skimmer, ultraviolet filter and activated carbon that should have been employed to support the action of the bacteria cannot be discontinued. However, if very few animals are kept, and large numbers of bacteria are present, it is possible to maintain healthy animals using only the subsand filter (and the necessary lighting). This situation can be more or less judged by the experienced aquarist who, nonetheless, will be on the alert to see if the withdrawal of apparatus leads to difficulties within his aquarium. There would seem to be little reason to remove important apparatus from an aquarium unless the aquarist is interested only in maintaining algae, or few animals or is displeased with its physical appearance.

The use of ozone is effective in controlling troublesome microorganisms in marine aquariums. It is a temptation to use this powerful tool when trouble develops. Because of numbers and kinds of organisms in an aquarium, amount of water present, size of bacterial populations, condition of organisms and other factors, different amounts of ozone must be used. Therefore, it is necessary to experiment by trial and error to see how much ozone should be used. This makes its use tricky and it is recommended that only the experienced aquarist use it. Its use probably should be limited to when there is a serious outbreak of disease and not on a continual basis.

Equipment for setting up aquarium

AQUARIUM
All glass
Water (natural or synthetic)

HOOD
Plywood (¼")
Nails

SPLASH PLATE
Plexiglas (⅜ or ¼")
Ethylene dichloride (for gluing)

FILTERS
Protein skimmer
Subsand (undergravel)
Sand (calcium parts of marine organisms, crushed oyster or clam shell, dolomite)
Ultraviolet (sterilizer type)
Activated carbon

AERATION
Air pump
Air tubing (¼")
Gang valve

ELECTRICAL
Fluorescent strip
Fluorescent bulb (s) ; GroLux or Plant Light
Toggle switch
Cord
Plug
Electrical tape (for splicing)

TOOLS
Hammer, saw, drill, knife

FEEDING
Frozen brine shrimp and common eating shrimp
Blender

MISCELLANEOUS
Rubber ball with hole and tube to fit (for use as syringe)
Flat object (plate) to prevent dislodging sand when filling

List of daily
observations

1. Check all airlift tubes to see that they are bubbling at about the same rate.
2. Check the bubbling rate of both the "return" and the main bubble column on the protein skimmer. Look carefully at the latter as it may be full of bubbles, but not densely packed with them.
3. Check to see the level of contaminants in the collecting cup of the protein skimmer.
4. Check to see that heater(s) is working properly. This can be done by watching to see if the indicator light goes on, if a shimmer appears adjacent to the heating element, or by temporarily turning the dial to a higher setting and then adjusting it back when the heater starts.
5. Check to see that the light is operating.
6. Check to see that the ultraviolet filter is operating.
7. Check for obviously sick or dead fish and other organisms—count the number of fish that are present to see if any are missing.
8. Watch behavior of individual fishes for some minutes to see if normal.
9. Watch to see if most of the food is eaten after fish are fed.
10. Watch progress of algal buildup (when aquarium is new) .

WEEKLY OR BIMONTHLY OBSERVATIONS
1. Check for buildup of salt deposits anywhere beneath or outside hood.
2. Remove any spray or salt deposits from light or bulb in the ultraviolet filter.
3. Check water level and add, if necessary.

List of readings

BOOKS

Axelrod, Herbert R., and Vorderwinkler, W. (Rev. ed.) *Salt-Water Aquarium Fish.* Jersey City, N.J.: TFH Publications, 1972, 349 pp. (illustrated). Gives particulars on different marine species that will help the aquarist.

Cox, Graham F. *Tropical Marine Aquaria.* New York: Grosset and Dunlap, 1972, 155 pp. (illustrated.) Mostly facts on tropical marine organisms with general information on aquarium keeping.

Sindermann, Carl J. *Principal Diseases of Marine Fish and Shellfish.* New York: Academic Press, 1970 (illustrated). A treatise giving detailed information on many diseases. It is somewhat technical.

Spotte, Stephen H. *Fish and Invertebrate Culture: Water Management in Closed Systems.* New York: John Wiley and Sons, 1970, 145 pp. (illustrated). An important book giving detailed information on the mechanisms of achieving good water quality. It is somewhat technical.

Straughan, Robert P. L. (2nd rev. ed.) *The Salt-Water Aquarium in the Home.* New York: A. S. Barnes and Co., 1969, 355 pp. (illustrated). General information on keeping aquariums—mostly facts on various marine organisms that can be kept.

Valenti, Robert J. *The Salt-Water Aquarium Manual.* New York: Aquarium Stock Co., 1968 (illustrated). Information on keeping marine aquariums—mostly facts on various marine organisms.

OTHER PUBLICATIONS

Books and Articles About the Sea. Miami, Fla.: Wometco Miami Seaquarium. A series presenting lists of interesting books and articles about marine organisms and other subjects related to marine aquarium keeping.

Sea Frontiers. Miami, Fla.: International Oceanographic Foundation. Excellent periodical giving information about marine organisms and many other subjects related to the sea.

Tropical Fish Hobbyist. Jersey City, N.J.: TFH Publications, Occasional informative articles about marine tropical fishes.

Index